Performing the Word

Preaching as Theatre

Jana Childers

Abingdon Press
Nashville

PERFORMING THE WORD
PREACHING AS THEATRE

Copyright © 1998 by Abingdon Press

This book is printed on elemental-chlorine–free paper.

Library of Congress Cataloging-in-Publication Data

Childers, Jana.
    Performing the Word : preaching as theatre / Jana Childers.
        p.   cm.
    Includes bibliographical references.
    ISBN 0-687-07423-1 (alk. paper)
    1. Preaching.   I. Title.
    BV4211.2.C464   1998
    251—dc21   98-28390
                                                                       CIP

Unless otherwise noted, Scripture quotations are from the New Revised Standard Version Bible. Copyright 1989 by the Division of Christian Education of the National Council of the Churches of Christ in the USA. Used by permission.

Scripture quotations noted KJV are from the King James Version of the Bible.

"The Word" from *For Heaven's Sake: A Musical Revue*, by Helen Kromer. © 1961 by Helen Lenore Kromer. © 1963 (new material added) by Walter H. Baker Co. Used by permission of Baker's Plays.

00 01 02 03 04 05 06 07—10 9 8 7 6 5 4 3 2

MANUFACTURED IN THE UNITED STATES OF AMERICA

To my directors

M. James Young,
W. J. Beeners,
and
Wayne R. Rood

With gratitude

Contents

Preaching and theatre share a great deal of ground, whether we care to admit it or not. Though the terrain where rhetoric and preaching meet is exceedingly well trod and the intersection of literary criticism's concern with homiletics' concern has been carefully mapped, the vast, fertile country where preachers and actors may tip back their chairs in the sun and enjoy what the other knows is largely unexplored. We preachers have not, in fact, cared to admit that it is a territory that has anything much to do with us. We know a dubious neighborhood when we see it and we are happy with our own little zip code. We will gerrymander the district, if necessary, to keep it out.

If we were to organize an expedition into such territory, we would have to set aside a couple of fears and one or two key misconceptions. We would have to accept the burden of a few fat questions. And it would help if we could muster a better reason to face the climb than that "it's there."

This book wants to encourage the reader in all those things. I hope we will be able to make a rudimentary map, start a discussion, and let go of a few inhibitions along the way. But most of all, I hope that those who take the trip will discover some new, useful muscles and a richer supply of oxygen to fuel their efforts.

My own foray into the world of the arts began twenty-five years ago, and it saved my life. If it didn't literally save my biological life, it did save my soul. Raised within the narrow walls of mid-twentieth-century American Pentecostalism, I was choking for air when I met M. James Young in the fall of 1972. The aperture he opened for me was larger than the proverbial window—a double-wide cosmic garage door, perhaps. The universe loomed, it seemed to me, on the other side.

I suppose I had thought of "art" before in terms of decoration. Rococo motifs and colored paper streamers were equally uninteresting to me. Under Professor Young's auspices I came to see art as a way of making sense, a way of making meaning, a way of having both the bedrock of faith and the spiritual lava I needed. In art, and in theatre in particular, a young Christian girl didn't have to choose between head and heart, orthodoxy and ecstasy. You could have them both. Theatre delights in juxtaposition, ambiguity, and tensiveness.

During the three decades since I began my own pilgrimage, preaching and the arts have been making a long slow move in each other's direction. Theologians Paul Tillich and Harvey Cox nudged from one angle, homileticians Charles Rice and Eugene Lowry from another. Paul W. F. Harms and Leroy Kennel advocated for "drama" in preaching. First-person sermons gained popularity; bathrobes and sandals found their way into the pulpit.

Seminaries began to see the value of teaching "drama skills" to their students. W. J. Beeners built a studio in the upper reaches of an Irish Gothic building on the campus of Princeton Theological Seminary and began hiring instructors from the New York stage and from the prestigious regional theatre, the McCarter, located just across the street. On the West Coast, Wayne Rood directed plays at the Pacific School of Religion, founded the Bay Area Religious Drama Service, worked with artists at *intersection*, a San Francisco project for religion and the arts, and joined forces with scholars Jane Daggett Dillenberger and John Dillenberger at the new Graduate Theological Union. In New York, Union Theological Seminary hired the accomplished actor Robert Seaver to work with its budding preachers.

The religious drama movement, already being funded in several places by Rockefeller money, gave preaching what was perhaps the biggest nudge of all. In the sixties, the National Council of Churches sponsored "The Religious Drama Workshop," bringing together such great figures of church and theatre as Harold Ehrensperger, Argyle Knight, Blaine Fister, Kay Baxter, Robert Seaver, E. Martin Browne, Jim Warren, and Jim Young. When funding for such events ran out in the seventies, "Ecumenical Council on Drama and the Arts" was born. Headquartered in St. Louis, it subsisted, in the time-honored tradition of the theatre, on a shoestring. During this time also, the professional association of theatre educators, ATHE, responded to the growing interest by forming a religious drama subgroup. And in the eighties CTA, Christians in the Theatre Arts, was founded. As the church-and-theatre movement peaked and settled, the gap slowly closed between preaching and its cognate art.

Preaching had been going through its own changes. The kerygmatic preaching of the sixties gave way in the seventies to an interest in inductive preaching. The eighties brought an emphasis on narrative and imagination. By the nineties few people were shocked when preaching was referred to as an art. An interest in performative speech, spurred by the insightful work of Charles L. Bartow and Richard Ward, was growing, leaving little to keep an impertinent young West Coast homiletician from raising the question of preaching's consanguinity with theatre.

This book is my attempt to start a conversation about preaching and its closest cousin. I approach the intersection between preaching and theatre as a student of the art of theatre, an actor and director myself, as one who holds a high view of theatre's art, but most of all as a homiletician. The questions raised here come not from the point of view of a cultural anthropologist or a dramaturge; they are not prompted by or pursued under the auspices of the performance studies movement. I raise these questions as a preacher and an actor who sees a kinship between her arts.

I am painfully aware that some of the language that is helpful to me in this enterprise—a word such as "performance," for example—is foreign and even offensive to church folks. I hope the arguments presented here will help to redeem such language from the unnecessarily negative connotative use that has become so common in the church, and that the lexicon of theatrical language employed here will be useful to homileticians in talking about what we have euphemistically called the "delivery" end of preaching. Most of all, I hope that those who enter the conversation will discover the kind of fresh air I discovered in Jim Young's theatre all those years ago.

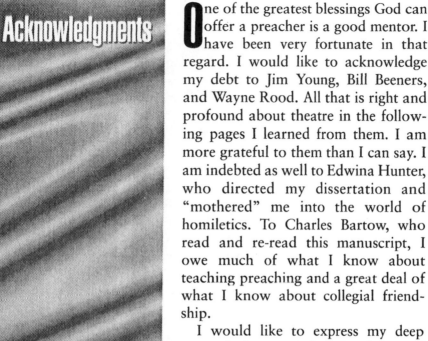

Acknowledgments

One of the greatest blessings God can offer a preacher is a good mentor. I have been very fortunate in that regard. I would like to acknowledge my debt to Jim Young, Bill Beeners, and Wayne Rood. All that is right and profound about theatre in the following pages I learned from them. I am more grateful to them than I can say. I am indebted as well to Edwina Hunter, who directed my dissertation and "mothered" me into the world of homiletics. To Charles Bartow, who read and re-read this manuscript, I owe much of what I know about teaching preaching and a great deal of what I know about collegial friendship.

I would like to express my deep appreciation to the Academy of Homiletics for their support and, in particular, to my friend and homiletical compatriot Lucy Rose. Lucy's death in July 1997 deprives us not only of an honest, insightful, original thinker but of the beloved Big Sister of a generation of women homileticians.

There are two volumes that have inspired and informed my interest in preaching and the art of theatre and that have been more than books to me: Alla Bozarth-Campbell's *The Word's Body: An Incarnational Aesthetic of Interpretation* (1979) and Charles L. Rice's *The Embodied Word* (1991). I am also grateful for the encouragement of three congregations, the

Pluckemin Presbyterian Church of Pluckemin, New Jersey; Grace Presbyterian Church of Wichita, Kansas; and the First Presbyterian Church of San Anselmo, California. They have been generous to a fault with me. Their witness to the transforming power of Jesus Christ has encouraged me to believe what I teach.

I owe thanks as well to the San Francisco Theological Seminary, for the generous sabbatical leave that made this work possible. And to my colleagues at SFTS, especially Browne Barr, Lewis Rambo and Warren Lee, who possess the spiritual gift of encouragement and who have lavished that gift on me, I am very grateful.

If I have been well blessed with mentors and friends, my family represents an embarrassment of riches. My parents, Jim and June Childers, raised me in the knowledge of God and the love of the Scripture. It is no small advantage to be born of the union of a church pillar and a prayer warrior. Undergirded by their love and faith, my life has been spiritually privileged from its beginnning. When people respond positively to my preaching, I often wonder just how much of the credit is attributable to the force of my mother's prayers.

Finally I would like to offer thanks to God for the support of my husband, Gary Dreibelbis. I am grateful for the long hours in my study that he did not begrudge, the wise council that he did not insist I take, and the too-short vacations that he did not resent. I did not know what a great thing I was doing when I married him. I know now.

Chapter One

Toward a Lively Homiletic

The house was packed. I should know; I was standing next to the last pew, shoe-horning people in. Too restless to sit anyway, I carried on a nonverbal conversation with some of my rowdier friends crammed together in the back row. They were antsy too, shifting to find a comfortable perch on the top of the pew back. It was not just us. The whole crowd rippled and rustled, unused to the numbers and the room temperature, excited by the occasion.

A choir of Korean students and their families in the neon colors of traditional dress sang, flat out, their hearts in their faces. The dance elements they wove into their anthems made my stomach mambo and my toes slide around in my shoes. For a fraction of a moment, I felt as if I could speak Korean. I was glad, very glad, that I had an excuse to be standing.

He slipped into the pulpit. A medium-sized black man with a Smile and a self-effacing manner. Laying his head to the side briefly, his body weaving subtly, he complimented the choir. He was glad, he said, for the opportunity to feel kinship with another tradition that—like his own—could move so joyously. The Smile was a beam. We were caught up in it; we took it in. The sermon hadn't even started yet.

He picked up the Bible and you could feel the congregation rise in their seats to meet him. Some bodies actually leaned forward, eyes darting, then honing in on the pulpit. Others gripped the arm rest or an available hand. Nobody looked away. "Yes, then what?" ran through the corporate consciousness over and over, as the story poured out.

His voice played through us and in us. It was like a train that carried us along we knew not where. It slowed and quickened, rose, fell, and paused uncannily. It worked in trio: the comfortable, large movements of his arms, the intensity of his thought, and the singing words swirling together.

It began to be clear he had our number. We were tickled and challenged, amused and disturbed. He addressed himself first to one side of us, then the other, circling in and bearing down. More and more we felt that he *saw* us, this guest preacher from the other side of the country—he knew a part of us we had kept hidden lately, that we'd half forgotten about. Little by little it dawned on us: this was a *good* part of us—we were proud of this once; we could be again—why have we been playing small, hiding our light? Our laughter roared up larger and larger. Heads shook, wry smiles spread.

We were ready to sober down when the moment came. As he unfolded the text's crucial scene, the motion picture screens inside each mind rolled on in technicolor. The biblical landscape had never seemed so close, so compelling. I remember thinking I'd never found that character so sympathetic before. His voice led us on, led us down inside ourselves, led us toward each other. We faced ourselves.

Relief was palpable. After a beat, his voice picked up and glided on. We settled in. A couple of my friends slid down from the pew back; a few folks crossed their arms, face muscles relaxed. We followed him gladly from pause to pause, filling in with our own thoughts, our own feelings, snapshots from our own lives. Rabbit trails offered themselves, and we ignored them—this was more interesting, and it was more satisfying for us to be together in it like this. We had faced the worst and stood it. Another way had been provided. We would have been happy to go on and on.

Need I tell you that it was an evening that those in attendance will always remember? Would you be surprised to hear that afterward people spoke of the Holy Spirit sweeping through the room? Would you find it hard to believe that many thought the forty-five-minute sermon too short—that Presbyterians wept, Episcopalians clapped, and academicians were speechless?

Later that week, I wrote to the preacher whose sermon had so affected my life and the life of my community. Trying to express how exalting the experience had been for me as a believer and how sobering it had been for me as a preacher, I stumbled on, searching for something intelligent to say about his pulpit skills.

I could not identify the crucial ingredient that made that sermon different from other effective sermons. I had to say something that feels a bit like cheating to an academician. I had to say what was the only thing I could imagine that could account for such an experience. In frustration, I abandoned homiletical analysis, my usual stock in trade, and blurted out the truth on the page. "Apparently, the Holy Spirit is much more willing to be stirred up than I had previously believed," I said, wondering even as I wrote the words what I could say to my students about HOW such a thing happens.

••• PREACHING: THE OPEN VOLCANO •••

Responsible teachers are careful not to claim too much for their art. For homileticians, even more than for some of our brothers and sisters in other theological disciplines, it is important to stay humble. God has been known to overwhelm us. God has even been known to stand us up. God has her own ideas about what makes for a powerful sermon and some of them have yet to be revealed.

The poet-theologian Amos Wilder says that going to church should be like "approaching an open volcano where the world is molten and hearts are sifted. The altar is like a third rail that spatters sparks; the sanctuary is like the chamber next to an atomic oven: there are invisible rays and you leave your watch outside."[1] Presumably, preaching should be something like this too—or at least should participate in the process. Wilder's image is an effective reminder of the ultimate mystery and unpredictability of preaching—and of its potential power.

The question of where in contemporary preaching that electric, volcanic, atomic, life-changing power may be found is a troubling one. How is it that so much preaching seems weak and watery or dead and flat? Richard Lischer points to a "theological homelessness," which has diminished preaching's substance, coherence, authority, and relevance.[2] Others have mentioned shifting attitudes toward authority,[3] a suspicion of institutions,[4] and a change in the consumer's "palate" brought on by the conditioning effects of a multimedia culture.[5] Postmodernism has also been examined in the search for culpability.[6] Slowly, homileticians are building answers. There is still more uncertainty than there is consensus. However, it is worth noting that when questions about what is missing in contemporary preaching are put to laypeople, they yield an age-old and surprisingly consistent response: passion.

Call it passion, life, authenticity, naturalness, conviction, sincerity, or being animated. Call it fire, sparks, electricity, mojo, spiritual lava, or juice. It is what listeners want in a preacher. "We want our preacher to preach like he believes what he's saying," says a pastoral search committee. "We don't like ministers who read their sermons," says another. "If our preacher would only speak to us from her heart, . . . " says a member.

Preachers know this, of course, and are understandably torn. On one hand they see real reason for caution. To misjudge the line between authenticity and histrionics is to make the most embarrassing mistake imaginable. Sometimes it's worse than embarrassing; a miscalculation in this area can damage the trust-relationship between preacher and listener. Worse still, such experiences have been known to put some listeners off preaching for life. Who has not seen a preacher "go overboard" and cringed? Who cannot call to memory the picture of a television evangelist—tears coursing, glasses fogging, lip dripping, and handkerchief mopping? Who can be blamed for wanting to give that spectacle a wide berth?

On the other hand, many preachers feel the pull to be more . . . something. They castigate themselves, "If only I could get away from my manuscript." Some experience a sense of restlessness, "Maybe I should try to get down out of the pulpit and walk among the people." Some blame themselves: "If I were wittier, a better storyteller, less inhibited, more energetic, sexier. . . ."

WHAT MAKES A SERMON SPECIAL?

Toward a Lively Homiletic

What is it that makes a sermon work, fly, come to life, have zing, take wing, tear the place up? What gets a sermon up off the page, across the tops of the pews, and down into people's insides? What gives preaching transconscious appeal—the kind of impact that affects not just cerebrum but cerebellum too? What is the difference between that kind of sermon and the one that seems to dribble down the front of the pulpit and out into the aisles?

Those of us who work in the academic discipline of homiletics have plowed the ground of several fertile fields, looking for answers. We have corrected and recorrected the course: logical coherence versus excessive rationality, deductive versus inductive method, evocative versus discursive language, rhetorical agenda versus theological agenda, and rhetorical mode versus narrative mode, not to mention a host of overlapping and sometimes competing hermeneutical techniques. We have wrestled the sermon out of the volcano's mouth and onto the examination table. We have strapped it down. Perhaps we shouldn't be too surprised that it has stopped wiggling.

It is not, of course, the examination or the plowing or the course correcting that is the problem. Homileticians, like other scholars, are only doing what needs to be done—and are often doing it rather well. Academicians of faith have believed for centuries that "all truth is God's truth and all beauty is God's beauty." There is no reason to fear that God's truth will be damaged or God's sensibilities offended by honest human attempts to understand what is understandable. No, it's not the attempt to understand that is the problem. But there might be a problem with the flatness.

In order to get our fingers on this thing, to see its distinctive and constituent features and identify its distinctive and constituent parts, we have had to lay it out flat. We needed to see it on the page, didn't we? We had to lay it out flat, and we had to hold it still. This need to stop-motion the sermon in order to study it has affected homileticians working on methodology not only in the privacy of our own studies but often in our classrooms and pulpits as well.

Every semester I explain to my students that I don't necessarily want them to become manuscript preachers; I require them to sub-

19

mit a manuscript before they preach as a kind of pedagogical necessary evil. In order to make accurate observations about the effectiveness of their transitions, their use of evocative language and approach to the biblical text, I need to take a close look at what they plan to do. I promise them that there are some things I can do to help them with reanimating the sermon, all the while knowing that, in many cases, it won't be enough. Once the sermon has become ink, it can be difficult to turn it back into blood.

Contemporary homileticians are like watchmakers who have taken apart the timepiece, discovered which gears are defective, and reassembled the innards only to find that we can't get the thing ticking again. We are like field scientists who have figured out a way to subdue the volcano and get inside. Once there, we sit dangling our feet from a ledge halfway down, waiting for something to bubble.

••• THE PECULIARNESS OF PREACHING •••

The stop-motion study of preaching has come up short for a good reason. The flat-on-the-table examination of sermons has proved frustrating too, also for reasons that make sense. *Preaching is by its very nature an event.*[7] Preaching is something happening. It is more process than document, more experience than artifact, more volcano than igneous rock. A sermon that is read is not without value, but it is not preaching—it is devotional literature. For just this reason, many a preacher has felt ambivalent about allowing her or his sermon to be transcribed and distributed in written form. What is true for a good joke is true for preaching as well: for many good sermons "you had to be there." In addition, *preaching is a corporate event,* which does not mean that it cannot also be deeply personal.[8] Part of the peculiar alchemy of preaching—the thing for which "you had to be there"—is the way in which listeners sitting in the same room, focused on the sound of the same human voice, are wound together. The energy of the sermon ebbs and flows in concert with the coming-together of the listeners. However one may understand the source and orchestration of sermon energy, the congregation's participation is an essential ingredient in that mix. Their presence makes the corporate event of preaching a live and living event—an event that transpires between and among people.

[*Preaching is also a transforming[9] event* that interprets sacred texts. The interpretation process acts on the preacher and the listeners. As they bring themselves to the biblical text, they are changed.] As they offer themselves, stand before the text, and open themselves to its images, transformation becomes possible. This transformative action may be seen to work in a circulating, back-and-forth pattern. The reader of the text (preacher or listener) alternately wills herself to set herself aside (kenosis) in order to listen to the text, and lets herself bring the stuff of her life to the text (plurosis) in order to appropriate the text. In other words, the reader interprets the text both by submitting herself to it *and* by bringing herself to it. The former may be accomplished with the use of prayer or rigorous intellectual exercise, for example. The latter might be done by associating emotions, kinesthetic sensations, or visual memories with the text's images. More will be said about the workings of this process later (in chapter 4), but for now it is enough to observe that the transformative nature of preaching implies a certain level of dynamism—a certain kind of movement or life.

Preaching needs a language and a method that will take the full measure of its liveliness. Literary criticism, rhetoric and narrative theory have their place in homiletics; but they leave a strategically significant gap. Ultimately, they are insufficient to preaching's task. They cannot account for the three-dimensionality, the collaborative creativity, and the spiritual electricity that drive the preaching moment. Preaching is a peculiar, even unique, enterprise. It requires a language and method that can address what is distinctive about it: its life-changing, life-giving, life-building liveliness. Preaching needs a homiletic that can account for its peculiar life.

✦✦✦ AN ANTIDOTE TO DEADNESS ✦✦✦

Preaching is a theological event. Indeed, dictionary definitions identify homiletics as a branch of theology. However, over the years the relationship between the two disciplines has been understood in several different ways. It is in the peculiar dynamic between the two disciplines that a clue for a lively homiletic may be found. More than one homiletician has seen something familiar in the relationship: "Homiletics is to theology what rhetoric is to philosophy," I once heard Charles L. Bartow say. Others have pointed to the value of theology as a preacher's tool: "Theology is something you do on your way to the pulpit," contemporary theologian Benjamin Reist tells his classes. Still others have understood theology as that which provides preaching with a frame of reference or even a "check."

Few would quarrel with the assertion that the two fields belong to each other. But there is little consensus about who owns whom. Certainly, many have preached as though they believed that preaching derives from theology. The most enthusiastic of these can even be seen, on occasion, carrying phone-book—sized volumes of Barth and Calvin into the pulpit with them. Such preaching is often educational and can even be inspiring.[10] But doctrinal preaching is not the only place where theology may be seen to be important to preaching.

For example, theological reflection itself may be considered a mode of preaching. In addition, many preachers construct their sermons based on what might be called a theological diagnosis of their situation. Theological point of view obviously shapes hermeneutical and homiletical decisions. Even the preacher's understanding of his or her role and of the task of preaching itself are largely theological issues.

However, of all the ways in which theology interplays with preaching, perhaps the most striking centers on theology's lexicon. While it is not surprising that preachers use theological language to express their experiences with preaching, it is very interesting indeed that it doesn't stop there. Its usefulness is not limited to preachers' work. Theology's language system seems to be trying to point preaching beyond traditional homiletical boundaries.

Creation, Incarnation, Transformation, Epiphany, Illumination, Annunciation, Inspiration, Creative Spark, Spirit, Communion. This is the language not only of theologians but of artists. Theological language is the language of creativity. It provides vocabulary and categories for the expression of our experiences with the creative process. Such language suggests that preaching is part of a vast, generative world.

Theology prods homiletics to stretch its map. "Go on," theology encourages us, "explore this country. These people speak your language. Don't you see you are related to them?" Indeed, it is true. We are related. Theological language—creation language—is not the province of just theologians and preachers or even of people of faith alone. It may even be that it is used more frequently in some theatres and art classrooms than in some churches.

Just as preachers have been known to borrow the vocabulary of artists (some happily, some in spite of themselves), artists use theological language to describe their experience with the creative process. The parallels are especially striking between the preachers' vocabulary and that of their closest artistic cousins, actors. Even the most puritanical preacher may make occasional reference to the organist's "picking up cues" or to the chancel's "downstage" area. He or she may speak of "being present" in the preaching moment on a good Sunday, or of having "lost my rhythm" on a bad. Similarly, words such as "creation," "epiphany," "truth," and "incarnational" are heard frequently in acting classes and directors' studios. However, though preachers may use dramatic vocabulary quite lightly—more as a matter of convenience than conviction—the use of theological language to describe the creative process (in preaching, acting, painting, writing, and so forth) is hardly a casual thing.

Theological language is the language most appropriate to understanding the creative process because human creativity echoes Divine creativity. Dorothy Sayers' observations on the subject are among the best known. She sees resonance between the roles of the persons of the Trinity and key aspects of the creative process.[11] But her interest in such parallels is hardly unique. The work of numerous others, such great minds as Paul Tillich[12] and Jürgen Moltmann[13] among them, confirms connections between theology's agenda and art's and suggests that such connections are more than coincidental.[14]

For artists, words such as "creation," "revelation," and "incarnation" are not lightly borrowed jargon; they are words that describe the creative process in the most accurate and profound terms available. Such language fits human experience with creativity because the human experience in this regard so closely mirrors the divine. It might be said that the only language up to the task of elucidating artistic processes is theological language, because such processes are ultimately creative, that is, life-giving; and theological language is the language of genesis, death, and new life. The same kind of creation language (theological language) that helps artists articulate their experience helps preachers.

It is this lexicon, the vocabulary that preachers and artists hold in common, that points toward an antidote for preaching's deadness. When creation language is applied in a discussion of the nature of preaching, we are a step closer to a lively homiletic. We are able to see preaching as a creative act—an act that brings into being something that did not exist before. Such generative activity is necessarily active, lively, and life-giving.

••• AN ANTIDOTE TO FLATNESS •••

Not only does theology suggest a way for preachers to broaden their understanding of the nature of their task but it gives their preaching shape and depth. Preachers may be interested in many different performance techniques that counteract flatness in the pulpit (and we will examine some of them in the following chapters), but first among their friends in this regard is theology. No matter how good a preacher is at embodying a sermon—giving it life and shape through kinesthetic expression—a substanceless sermon cannot be disguised.

Theology reminds preaching of matters of ultimate importance. Animated preaching that deals with trivial matters is not lively preaching; it is preaching that lacks force. "French lacquer preaching," H. H. Farmer called it, "lacking depth and tenderness and searching power."[15] It is as if it doesn't have enough substance to get up off the page—it has to be scraped. Preaching that attends to theology's large themes will have the kind of *magnitude* required to make impact on a listener. It might even be said that theology provides preaching with a sense of *size*.

24

In a conference on preaching more than a decade ago, Fred Craddock made the point with characteristic modesty. He shared the floor that evening with a well-known preacher whose acerbic wit played perfectly off Craddock's drawling charm. North met south and Mutt met Jeff and the question and answer session hummed along. Time after gracious time the diminutive Southern gentleman yielded the floor to his tall, fast-talking colleague.

Finally, the question of theology's role in preaching came up and Craddock fielded the question. He took the occasion to compliment the New York preacher's work, allowing how it provided a fine example of a theologically informed style. "You know what I like about this guy's preaching?" Craddock drawled, looking up slyly at the towering figure, "It has size!"

Theology can do much to enlarge and protect preaching. It can enhance coherence and relevance in a sermon, provide it perspective, vouchsafe its integrity, and support its authority.[16] But at least as important as these is theology's ability to give preaching content. Theology can help keep preaching from being flat. It can prevent sermons from being the kind of thing that could just as well have been slipped quietly under the door in an envelope one night. It can make preaching as big, bulky, bumpy, and "weighty with Max Planck's quanta"[17] as are life's largest concerns.

Of course, that street goes both ways. Preaching does as much for theology as theology does for preaching in this regard. Theology and preaching exist in a dialectical relationship, one shaping the other, one helping to bring the other to expression. To tease them apart is a messy, unnecessary, and perhaps counterproductive task. They need each other. It is out of the relationship between preaching and theology that three-dimensional preaching emerges. Out of their synergy, substantial lively sermons are born.

There is no doubt that preaching contributes its share to the equation. It is preaching, after all, that supplies theology with the material it needs to do its business—the raw materials of life. What preachers dig out and offer up every Sunday morning tells the story of a particular group of God's faithful for a particular week. When it goes well, when text and context merge in event, what preachers dig out and offer up on a Sunday is human life with God's fingerprints all over it. It is the very material—life's humus—that theologians spend their lives hunting down. Preaching supplies theology with some of its best clues about God's working in human lives. You might even say that preaching, when it is done right, is theology's best resource for understanding God's way with us.

When theologians are especially good listeners, they may be reminded of something more—something that goes to the heart of the nature of their task. They may be reminded that the gospel is not primarily a black-print-on-white-paper event. Preaching may remind theology that the gospel is essentially an oral/aural event. The gospel, like preaching, is about the Word that gets inside us, that takes up dwelling in us; the Word that speaks and is spoken through human mouths; the Word that impregnates us through the ear.

The deal goes both ways, as we have said. Without theology, there would be nothing to keep contemporary preaching from passing wholesale into the realm of pop psychology, mysticism, moralism—of flatness. Without preaching, there would be nothing to get theology up off the page. Without preaching, theology wouldn't matter.

⚫⚫⚫ ABOUT THE NATURE OF PREACHING ⚫⚫⚫
↳ IT IS AN ACTIVE EVENT⏋

Preaching, by its very nature, is a lively event. It does all kinds of active things. It weaves among people, creating community. It puts people in a conversation with a text, a back-and-forth conversation that is more dance than conversation. It opens people up and changes their insides around. It creates.

Unlike devotional literature or inspiring short stories, it gets up off the lectern and takes on flesh. Unlike theology, it is not flat—not a blueprint. Preaching is theology's bustling house. It uses theology's language and rises to the occasion that is suggested by theology's scope. But it does all these things in a three dimensional and four/four time.

Preaching, by its very nature, is an off-the-page and into-the-air kind of an enterprise. It is eventful and generative. Theology is a substantial, shaping force. It can handle the life-and-death–sized themes that give preaching magnitude. It is out of the dance between preaching and theology that resources for a lively homiletic emerge.

❧❧❧ ABOUT THE PURPOSE OF PREACHING ❧❧❧

A lively homiletic, which does justice to both the movement and the three-dimensionality of preaching, needs more than a healthy theology to make it fly. It needs a sense of purpose. Through the ages, Christians have held an astonishing number of different views on the question of preaching's purpose. A brief overview will provide a reminder of some of the historically acceptable answers to the question, Why preach?

The early church preached with at least two different purposes and to two different audiences. Jewish Christian preaching, aimed at other Jews, tended to be exegetical in style. Its purpose was to place Jesus Christ in the context of Jewish Scripture. Gentile preaching of the same period addressed both Jews and Gentiles in a voice less concerned with exegesis and more concerned with repentance. Paul's sermon on Mars Hill exemplifies the Gentile approach to preaching.

In the first phase of the early church, the Gentile Christian preaching model was likely the more dominant of the two. However, as soon as Constantine's influence began to be felt, the popularity of the exegetical model soared, quickly outstripping the Gentile model. Gradually, a didactic approach entered the mix as the church found itself with a new generation to sustain.

It is this combination of models—exegetical preaching, preaching for conversion, and didactic preaching—along with the influence of classical rhetoric, that we see reflected in Augustine's (354-430) homiletic. Though not the first great Christian preacher recorded by history (note, for example, the prominence of Ambrose of Milan, 339-97, and his influence on Augustine), Augustine is the author of what is often thought of as the first textbook in homiletics, *On Christian Doctrine*. In the development of the Christian sermon, Augustine is not only an important mover and shaker but an important hinge. In him "we see the Latin sermon shed the Greek yoke and assume an original form."[18]

The form of preaching established by Augustine was to dominate much of Christianity well into the Middle Ages. It is a form that focuses on the interpretation of Scripture. For Augustine, the purpose of preaching may be understood in several ways. But perhaps his most common way of expressing the purpose of preaching was that of moving the hearer by way of the interpretation of Scripture. Preaching is about interpreting the tradition (Scripture) for the next generation, he believed. In testimony to the fact, the first three volumes of his four-volume work are devoted to the subject of hermeneutics.

It is important to note that although Augustine is known as a student of Ciceronian rhetoric (Cicero, 106-43 B.C., a distinguished Roman orator), his view of the purpose of preaching differs from the Ciceronian view. Though Augustine follows Cicero on the purposes of rhetoric (to teach, to delight, to persuade), when it comes to the subject of preaching, he transposes Cicero's language and adds an important caveat. The purposes of preaching are "to teach, to give pleasure and to move," Augustine states:

> If, however, the hearers require to be roused rather than instructed, in order that they be diligent to do what they already know, and to bring their feelings into harmony with the truths they admit, greater vigor of speech is needed. Here entreaties and reproaches, exhortation and upbraidings and all other means of rousing emotions are necessary.[19]

Augustine refines and expands the rhetorical notion that the purpose of preaching is *persuasion*. The purpose of preaching is a bit broader and deeper than the kind of rational persuasion that is classical rhetoric's goal. It has to do with moving the listener to be responsive to the unique authority of Scripture—or perhaps, moving the listener to be responsive by way of the unique authority of Scripture.

The notion that preaching had to do with this kind of "moving" brought about by conversion, interpretation, or teaching (or some combination of or variation upon these three) persisted into the Middle Ages. In the twelfth century Alan of Lille (1128-1202) articulated yet another alternative. For him the implied purpose of preaching might be called "formation." Preaching's work is seen as a lifelong process—a process Alan compares to climbing a ladder. Preaching sometimes addresses "holy things" and other times addresses practical matters of conduct, he says:

> Preachers are "angels" who "ascend" when they preach about heavenly matters and "descend" when they bend themselves to earthly things in speaking of behavior.[20]

Alan's understanding of preaching's purpose constituted a new category.

In the flow of preaching history, Alan of Lille is followed by a flood of cookbook-style texts that develop the "university sermon" (also called the scholastic sermon, this style of preaching is known for its rational appeals and intricate structure). These manuals typically prescribe six parts for the sermon: theme, protheme, repetition of theme, partition of theme, subdivision of theme, and amplification of each division. Practitioners of the university sermon understood the purpose of preaching in Aristotelian terms. That is, persuasion—a particularly rational flavor of persuasion—was the preacher's goal. Although the Reformation did much to overturn the dry style of the university sermon, Aristotle gained a foothold in Christian preaching that endures to this day. His hold on modern preaching is seen most strikingly in the seeming immortality of the three-point sermon and the persistent understanding of preaching as an enterprise that is primarily persuasive.

By the time of the Reformation, Christianity was ready for another revolution in preaching—and it got it. "Whatever else it was, the Reformation was a great preaching revival, probably the greatest in the history of the Christian Church."[21] Whereas pre-Reformation preachers had understood the goal of their work as persuasion (including conversion), interpretation, teaching, formation, or some combination thereof, Reformation preachers had their own ideas about the purpose of their work.

The importance of preaching to John Calvin's theology and ministry can hardly be overstated. With the help of the Holy Spirit's "spectacles," Calvin believed, preaching revealed the Word of God just as Scripture did. The sermon comprised the "outside" work of preaching, and the Holy Spirit supplied the "inside" work of illumination. The preacher's role in the process was to act as a "sign" through which God approaches people. In the course of a sermon on Deuteronomy 25, Calvin identifies the preacher's lips with the lips of Christ.[22]

It is possible from just these very few observations to see that, for Calvin, preaching's purpose is not limited to the abstract concept or to the rather wooden feeling that has often been associated with his use of the word "revelation." For Calvin the process is juicier than that. The purpose of preaching is revelation, but it is the kind of *revelation that comes in communing*. God "approaches," Christ is present, the Holy Spirit is illumining as the Word of God is revealed.

It was Martin Luther who developed the notion of preaching as "encounter," a notion reappropriated and popularized by twentieth-century neo-orthodoxy. Encounter or "that bodyless intersection where the divine and the human meet"[23] described both the purpose and nature of preaching. Certainly, preaching for Luther was not so much about telling the story of Jesus Christ (interpretation) or about holding Jesus Christ up as a moral example (formation). The purpose of preaching was "absorption." The preacher and the listener should be "absorbed" into Christ. Luther believed that in the act of preaching, a transaction occurred (something like what Calvin called "the wonderful exchange") whereby Christ is made present in the listener.

If the emphasis of Reformation preaching fell on preaching as a means of encountering God's presence, the emphasis of early Puritan preaching fell squarely on salvation. Of course, the message engendering conviction and faith was quickly followed by one of obedience and duty, those qualities more usually associated with Puritan piety. However, though Puritans clearly distrusted emotional appeals, the frequency of sermons that featured an excessively rational appeal has probably been over-emphasized.[24] By the seventeenth century we see again the pattern that was established in the early church; conversion (a type of persuasion) is the goal of preaching for a first generation of believers, but maintenance themes (teaching or formation) quickly develop and are identified by subsequent generations as preaching's *raison d'etre*. Indeed, we see the pattern repeated through the following centuries.

For Jonathan Edwards (1703-1758), conversion (persuasion) was the goal of preaching. By 1734, when revival fell upon Edwards' New England church, the influence of New England's Puritan ancestors had waned to the point that only 5 percent of Americans were members of a church.[25] This combined with an early eighteenth-century rush of immigration to create, in effect, a new generation of potential converts. Although revivalism did not start with Edwards, he became its chief apologist, defending its goals and methods against the academy's opposition. He proposed a model of the mind that stressed the interconnection of thought and emotion (in contrast to the rigid faculty psychology of his day). Edwards argued that the "sense of the heart" was the "spring" of conversion. He believed that individuals rationalized or justified what they already knew in their hearts to be true. The primary purpose of preaching was to persuade the heart, in the belief that the head would follow.[26]

On the question of preaching's purpose, nineteenth-century American theology falls along two lines of thought. In one, the revivalist movement, we can readily see the continuation of the conversion/maintenance cycle we have already identified. (For example, Wesley's staunch view of sanctification as a state of sinlessness is softened by Charles Finney in the succeeding generation to allow for a "second experience.") In the other, the rise of historical thinking leads to the creation of a new "tribe" of Christians who favor intuition over rationalism. These preachers concern themselves with such themes as human freedom (i.e., Unitarian preachers Channing, Emerson, and Parker in the first decade of the century), evidence an rising anthropology (i.e., Horace Bushnell, mid-century) and equate the kingdom of God with the Christianizing of American social life (i.e., Walter Rauschenbusch, at the end of the century).

In both strands, the general shift in preaching is away from the strong Calvinism of the eighteenth century (exemplified by Edwards' preaching) and towards more emphasis on the work (or the "freedom") of the human will. The moving of the will was understood as the purpose of preaching by both tribes of nineteenth-century America. Revivalists such as Charles Finney (1792-1875) and Phoebe Palmer (1807-1874) were primarily interested in moving the will for conversion. On the other side of the fence, Horace Bushnell (1802-1876) and his colleagues were aiming to move the will toward service. The intense interest of both tribes in the subject has had a lingering effect on the next several generations of preachers and may be seen even today in late-twentieth-century Madison Avenue-style appeals.

An alternative approach is represented by P. T. Forsyth (1848-1921), perhaps the best known of all "the preacher's theologians," sometimes called the first great evangelical of the twentieth century. Considered a forerunner of Karl Barth, it was Forsyth who coined the phrase "crisis theology." The objectivity of the Atonement and the necessity of its proclamation lie at the heart of Forsyth's theology. Forsyth held a sacramental view of the nature of preaching and understood preaching's purpose in terms of the "mediation" of the Word of God. He described the content of such mediation as personal, objective, and consistent with the nature of grace.

> Communion with God, the divine value of the soul, the development of all its powers, the fellowship of love, the joyful exchange of spiritual wealth, grateful delight in nature's good . . . such things are not heavenly ideals of ours but powers of God, already given.[27]

Forsyth's turn-of-the-century language may sound odd to the ear, but the goals he sets for preaching extend their fingers well down into twentieth-century homiletics.

Having lightly traced the question of preaching's purpose through church history, we see that preaching's goal has been defined in a wide variety of ways, including:

- demonstration of Christ's place in history
- repentance or conversion
- the instruction of the new generation
- the interpretation of Scripture
- to delight or give pleasure
- to move or be roused
- spiritual formation

- persuasion (some more rational, some less)
- revelation
- communion
- encounter
- absorption
- salvation
- obedience and duty
- revival
- to move the will toward conversion or service
- to mediate the Word of God

Most of these may be roughly categorized in three groups:
- persuasion
    - including repentance and conversion
    - rational conversion
    - emotional conversion
    - conversion of the will
    - demonstration of Christ's place
    - Augustinian notion of "moving"
    - salvation
    - revival
    - revivalist/social gospel preachers'
      - notion of moving the will

- maintenance
    - including teaching
    - formation
    - interpretation of Scripture
    - obedience and duty

- encounter with God
    - including revelation
    - mediation
    - communion
    - absorption

Although there is some flexibility and potential for overlapping in these groupings, and though it is far beyond the purview of this volume to demonstrate the relative dominance of one school, the rough pattern that is suggested here is an interesting one. Through the beginning of the twentieth century, persuasive appeals in their many and various forms (rational, emotional, or volitional) were a major force in preaching. Even what we have listed as maintenance models in many cases rely heavily on persuasive techniques. Though encounter models differ significantly from persuasion models in the way they prioritize experience over idea, they are not entirely free from persuasive appeals, either. And, although mid-century neo-orthodoxy refocused preachers' attention on encounter models and later-century transformational approaches[28] have shifted the homiletical agenda once again, the long reign of the persuasion model is far from over. Even at the end of the twentieth century, many preachers still preach as if listeners could be argued into the realm of God.

Among the problems with approaches that understand preaching's goal in terms of persuasion is a tendency to flatten and slow the preaching moment. Depth and girth, event and movement are often minimized. Instead of the glorious mountainous terrain of the kingdom of heaven, the listener gets the map—instead of the music video, the snap shot. At its worst, the persuasive approach restricts preaching's activity to the kind of the a-to-b movement of one person making a case to others, of ideas being broken apart, of principles applied, of concepts assembled, of human will being pressed, or of feelings being evoked from the listener.

If we conceive of preaching more as a creative event than a delivered message, the usefulness of the persuasive model is diminished. If we note that the scope and content of preaching is best suggested by theological categories, rhetorical models become less important. If we say that we believe that preaching is by nature a corporate and corporeal enterprise, then the limits of rational appeals are clear.

In contrast, the purpose of lively preaching might be described as facilitating openness: creating a space where the listeners can be open to change, shaping a moment when the congregation can say a yes or a no that comes from more than the cerebrum. The purpose of lively preaching might be illumination or encounter or epiphany. It might be absorption or communion or annunciation or transformation. What do lively sermons do? They open, draw, and hold people, creating a moment for God to move in.

❖❖❖ TOWARD A LIVELY HOMILETIC ❖❖❖

A lively homiletic should be able to do all the things that any homiletical model can do. It should have something to say about what preaching is, why we think we do it, how it interprets sacred texts, how it draws people in and holds them, and how it gets inside them. Though this book comments on all those things, the ideas here represent only the beginnings of such a model. The heart of this book is concerned with a corrective for one particular aspect of the preacher's experience. This book is about adding liveliness to all that is already solid and graceful in contemporary preaching.

The thesis of this chapter is that contemporary preaching has suffered from the fact that homileticians have sometimes paid more attention to sermon manuscripts than to sermons. I have suggested that theological language and reflection point us toward a bigger, livelier picture—a model of preaching that is by nature a creative event and whose purpose it is to open us to God's movement. Such a homiletic will need a method that can help preachers not only with words on a page but with performed words—the enlivened, embodied words that preach.

Chapter Two

Preaching as Theatre

Actors act and preachers preach. The words themselves are short and crisp, leaving little room for confusion: *act, preach.* Salt and pepper, bread and butter words, they are the kind that anybody might use. They are the kind of words that people *do* use every day, in fact, confident that they will be understood.

On the street, in the studio, in the pews there is not much confusion. Actors pretend and preachers scold. Actors mimic and preachers rhapsodize. Actors deceive and preachers lecture. While the two activities may be perceived to share a bit of ground (there is, for example, the common wisdom that "all preachers are frustrated actors"), the people in the pew do not want their preacher to act, and the folks on the far side of the proscenium arch do not want the actors to preach. In fact, poor preaching is "mere performance," and a play may flop if it is found to be "too preachy." The words are held apart. We know what we mean by these words, and we will brook no confusion.

It is the contention of this book that a little confusion in this area might, in fact, be good for the soul. As artists who operate in the mimetic/nemetic world (the world that both "imitates" and "dispenses" life), preachers and actors have much in common. And while the question of whether actors may wish to learn from preachers is an open one, best left to others to answer; the question about what preachers may learn from actors is tantalizing.

Why shouldn't one learn from the other? Theatre and preaching share the essential characteristics and qualities that can be said to be true of art in general: each probes for meaning; each is organic by nature; interest and integrity are requisite; distance plays a role; experience is the goal. In giving form to feeling,[1] art creates something that was not there before. It is mimetic, sometimes nemetic, and may be prophetic as well.

A chief characteristic of art is its ability to modify consciousness.[2] It does this in several ways, not all of them describable. One of the most important ways that art shapes perception and experience is through the use of imagery. From pictures and word-pictures to buildings, sonatas, and patterned textiles, artists present forms that "liberate perception . . . from all practical purposes, and let the mind dwell on the sheer appearance of things."[3] The artist knows how to use imagery to spark the viewer or reader or hearer to a new way of seeing. More than that, offering the audience a fresh set of images for their experience is offering them a chance to change. Art is "the making of images that trap imagination and so transform life."[4]

In addition to modifying consciousness, art evokes participation. It has drawing power. Like the other performance arts, preaching and theatre are collaborative and empathy-based. They have the power to create community and communion by drawing people together in a common response. In performance arts, a note is struck to which three hundred people may respond in the same way, a character is portrayed that hooks three hundred gizzards as one.

Not least among the similarities between theatre and preaching is the fact that they are often misunderstood in similar ways:

"Don't preach to me."

"He is merely acting."

"I don't need another sermon about this."

"It was all just a performance."

The words do not actually mean what they appear to mean. *Act, preach, perform.* They have been flattened in everyday use. *Acting* and *performance* are understood in terms of artifice. *Preaching* is understood in terms of persuasion. All are commonly *mis*understood. It may even be that they are misunderstood for some of the same reasons.

What has made it difficult for preachers to see our art as a performance art? What has kept us from admitting to the presence of the elephant in the room? Why have we limped along so long shuffling papers behind mammoth wooden desks? Why have so many seminaries offered their students the services of textual scholars and theologians but not of artists? Where are the classes in dance, oral interpretation, theatre, and choral music? We teach students to see in Scripture the written Word and to understand the public reading of Scripture as, in some sense, the spoken Word. What keeps us from teaching preaching as the performed Word?

In the church, the root of the problem is the understanding of *art* itself and of performance arts in particular. The arts have often been misunderstood by the church as educational tools and have been valued for their novelty or their ability to add force to a particular message. (This goes a long way toward explaining why theatre is so often the province of "the young people" in the church. It is thought to solve both of the church's chief problems with teenagers.) Does your church have a problem holding high school students' attention? Hire one of those national touring groups that does snappy skits with Christian morals. Are you looking for a way to get the history of the Reformation across? Borrow a few Geneva gowns and some false beards and let the kids put on a pageant. Is your pastor frustrated by the congregation's apathy toward abortion, or gay and lesbian rights, or drug abuse? Do what the medieval church did, produce a morality play.

The problem is that art is not concerned with education and entertainment, and it certainly does not deal with life in cut and dried terms. Other things are and do, and they may be valuable to the church but they are not art. In using the arts, or what it thinks of as art, in this way the Church unwittingly reinforces its own problem. Those of us who attend chancel dramas that hammer home the message with a ham-sized fist are confirmed in our suspicions that there is something inauthentic about this "art." Even if we can't put our fingers on it, we know it doesn't ring true. We feel manipulated. We feel something was "false" about our experience, and we are right.

Many faithful people for whom the word *art* raises a red flag are not thinking about art at all. They are thinking about experiences they have had with kitch or propaganda—with the gratuitous, the trivial, the sentimental or the manipulative. Art that deserves to be called art "does not teach, it reveals. It is not about lessons, but illumination; not about persuasion, but epiphanies; not about decision, but discovery. Art does not aim at entertainment, but pleasure."[5] Art operates not through coercion or falseness or the purveying of pat answers, but through precisely their opposites: art uncovers ambiguities in hopes of pointing to truth. While it may have the effect of entertaining or educating us along the way, it is not constructed for those purposes. If in fact it bends our arms or whitewashes our world, it is not art.

Art has a bigger agenda in mind. In it the stuff of human life, in all its ambiguity and complexity, is represented and transcended. Under its auspices, experiences that out-distance rational thought are born. Whereas argument depends on belief to be persuasive, theatre and preaching are not necessarily so limited. Art is uniquely able to facilitate encounter and engender belief. Early twentieth-century theatre critic Arthur Hopkins speaks not only for theatre artists but for many preachers as well. "In the theatre, I do not want the emotion that rises out of thought," he says, "but thought that rises out of emotion."[6]

If performance (or theatre) is defined with this view of art in mind, then it is easy to see that, far from being about deception or coercion, it aims at truth. Likewise, if we understand preaching as "art" in this sense, preaching will never be about scolding or lecturing or even about persuasion in the merely rational sense of the word. Seeing preaching and theatre in artistic terms is not the same thing as seeing them in namby-pamby terms, of course. That neither one can be defined in terms of arm-twisting or black-and-white categories does not mean that they lack force. Action, in fact, is key to both.

✦✦✦ THE ROLE OF ACTION ✦✦✦

Drama and homiletics each have at their root the agonistic. The English words *act, agitate,* and *agony* are derived from the same

Indo-European base *ag-*, "to drive." From this also comes the Latin *agere*, "to do." While theatre is widely understood as actors acting, it may be surprising to some to hear that there is anything active— let alone agonistic—about the pulpit-bound act of preaching. We will come to an examination of preaching's action in a moment, but let us look first at how the concept undergirds all that is important to the theatre.

Action has long been understood as theatre's essence. According to Aristotle, all literary and dramatic arts are concerned with the subject. Though various arts may be distinguished from one another by differences in manner (or convention), the object of each is the same—action. Each holds the mirror up to life, to a life that is moving. Since Aristotle, it has been said that theatre "imitates action."

It is important to note that Aristotle uses the terms *imitation* and *action* in ways that broaden their surface meanings. *Imitation* is not a question of superficial copying, for Aristotle, but of representation. What is represented in the arts might be described as "the form of the life of the spirit."

What shows up—what is represented—in Aristotle's famous mirror is the otherwise unseeable, the life of the spirit. The life of the spirit is a life full of choices and conflict, desires and designs. In short, it is an active life, not a still life that is reflected.

Just as Aristotle's use of *imitation* varies from everyday use, so his definition of *action* differs from the familiar definition. The *Poetics* uses the term not so much in its physical or literal sense but as it relates to motive. *Action,* for Aristotle, has to do with what Dante called the movement-of-spirit, the outward working of psychic or spiritual energy. "It may be described metaphorically as the focus or movement of the psyche toward what seems good to it at the moment."[7]

It is this understanding of action that led Aquinas to conceive of God as "pure act." And it is action in this sense that is crucial to both theatre and preaching. Richard Boleslavsky, the acting teacher who is responsible for disseminating much of the great Constantin Stanislavski's work, that is, for helping to perpetuate what became the famous "Method" school of acting, provides an example of how important it is for a director to identify the action of a play correctly. His observations apply as well to a preacher engaged in the task of interpreting a text. Boleslavsky compares the director's idea of the action of a play to the trunk of a tree, the leitmotif in music, and the poet's thought in a sonnet. Action is that which drives the play forward.

> The *Taming of the Shrew* is a play where two people long to love each other in spite of their impossible characters, and succeed in their longing. It might also be a play about a man who triumphs over a woman by "treating her rough." It might be a play about a woman who makes everybody's life miserable. . . . In the first case, the action is to love; in the second, swash-buckling; in the third, the anger of a vixen.[8]

The kind of assessment that Boleslavsky describes is just the kind that a preacher must apply to the biblical text. More than that, it is the very thing that makes the vital connection between an "arrested performance"[9] and a live one. The sermon must move, must be driven the way the text is. It is imperative that a preacher approach the text with questions of this kind:

> *What gets the Psalmist from "The Lord is the strong-hold of my life" to "Do not cast me off" and back to "Wait for the Lord"? (Psalm 27)*

> *What propels the narrator through the segue so that the picture on the listeners' mental screens shifts from the King's throne to his door? "Now the queen, by reason of the words of the kings and his lords, came into the banquet house." (Belshazzar's feast, Daniel 5:10, KJV)*

> *What drives Paul on from "We know that all things work together for good to them that love God." to "What shall we then say to these things?" to "For I am persuaded . . . "? (Romans 8:28-38, KJV)*

These questions lead the preacher to identify the action of the text and begin to see how the action of the sermon must take shape. In this sense, then, it is clear that the theatrical notion of action is applicable to preaching. Actually this understanding of action may be seen to undergird preaching in at least three important ways. First, preaching interprets conflict-laden texts and applies them to conflict-laden situations. The birth, death, and resurrection narratives, which are the focus of Christian preaching and which gave rise to the early medieval passion plays, are every bit as conflictual as the Dionysian dythrambs from which sprang Greek theatre. The cosmic struggle between life and death forms the spine of every Christian sermon; the personal struggle with good and evil fleshes out each moment in the pulpit.

The point was made with more rhetorical flair (and a bit more bite) at the end of the second century by the early church father Tertullian.

> If the literature of the stage delight you, we have literature in abundance of our own—plenty of verses, sentences, songs, proverbs; and these not fabulous, but true; not tricks of art, but plain realities. Would you have also fightings and wrestlings? Well, of these there is no lacking, and they are not of slight account. Behold unchastity overcome by chastity, perfidy slain by faithfulness, cruelty stricken by compassion, impudence thrown into the shade by modesty: these are contests we have among us, and in these we win our crowns. But would you have something of blood too? You have Christ's.[10]

Whatever view of preaching we accept, it must account for the tremendous energy implied by such contests. The importance of action in preaching may also be seen in the increasing popularity of the conflict-resolution format. The long reign of the "three points and a poem" style of preaching has come to an end. One of the complaints against the three-point sermon was about its inertia. Some congregations experienced such sermons as flat or static. Little movement is implied in such a format. No significant momentum may be gathered. It is difficult for the preacher to orchestrate one fluid, continuous movement of experience for the congregation when he or she is using a format that Fred Craddock has described as "three trips down the hill."

During the 1980s, such discontent with the three-point sermon combined with the influence of narrative theology to bring about a shift of focus in preaching. Emphasis in the teaching and practice of preaching moved away from the deductive, discursive style of preaching that had dominated mid-twentieth-century Christian worship, and toward something called *narrative preaching*.

Narrative preaching may be seen as action oriented, in that it leads a congregation through an experience of conflict to its resolution. Preaching in this mode means, or often means, moving the hearers from a sense of disequilibrium to equilibrium. Such a movement is said to take place along a plot line. Eugene Lowry, the homiletical father of the narrative sermon, defines it as one "in which the arrangement of ideas takes the form of a plot involving a strategic delay of the preacher's meaning."[11] Narrative preaching is agonistic or action-oriented in that its goal is to **move** the congregation from idea A to idea B, through an experience of suspense. The conflict posed and resolved lends movement to the sermon even as it creates and maintains the congregation's interest. Narrative preaching specializes in making ideas move. Its popularity has boosted the action quotient of the average contemporary sermon.

However, action is not the province of any one mode of preaching. Charles Rice, an early proponent of the artistic view of preaching, sees action in all kinds of preaching. "The sermon is where the action is," he says.[12] Don Wardlaw goes farther. "The sermon is unfolding action that implies ideas and is controlled by ideas; but the sermon is not primarily unfolding ideas."[13] The sermon *is* action. It is action that takes its direction from the flow of the life of the biblical text. It is action that *moves* the text's imagery, threading biblical images together with the stuff of the listeners' lives.

Preaching is an act. "Christ spoke far less of love than he practiced it," P. T. Forsyth says. "He did not publish a new idea of the Father—rather He was the first true Son. Christ as God's revelation is God's act; and our conveyance of Christ in preaching is Christ's act."[14] Sermons are act, active and action. They move or they ought to. They weave together—not just ideas but spirits. The essence of preaching is to be found in this action.

Finally, not only do both theatre and preaching deal with conflict and the action it generates, but both reflect upon it. Theatre's reflexive function is linked to its "doubleness,"[15] that is, theatre is "twice-behaved" or rehearsed behavior, giving it the ideal amount of distance from life's conflicts, optimizing perception. In a similar way, preaching's reflexive function may be seen to derive from its "tripleness"—or perhaps its "double doubleness." Preachers believe that distance is built in to both sides of their equation; they have distance from life's struggles and distance from the texts they interpret.

It is as if preachers hold one large mirror up to nature **and** a foggy, little pocket-sized one off at another angle, hoping for a glimpse of something Else. When such a glimpse is possible, what we are perceiving is more than human life. Encounter is enabled and preaching may be understood to have a nemetic as well as a mimetic function. That is to say that when both mirrors are functioning, a directness or a dealing out (nemesis) or a dispensing (nemein) of something—as well as imitation of something—may be seen. What is dispensed may not be nameable. We may categorize it as "ineffable" or "Other."

Contemporary preachers may yearn to enable such an encounter, but it is not their province alone. In the late twentieth century, it may even be the case that mimesis and nemesis come together more often in the theatre—especially in the theatres of those who hold a high and holy view of their art.[16] It is from such artists that preachers may well wish to learn.

In summary, we have identified action as the first of three important characteristics that are shared by theatre and preaching. Their agonistic character gives rise to a sense of movement, draws and maintains the audience's interest, and under the best circumstances, makes encounter possible. For this reason it is not difficult to understand how Moliere could say that he needed only "a board and a passion or two" for theatre—just enough conflict to draw the audience in and enough space to permit a little back-and-forth, a little cat-and-mouse playing with them. We have considered the conflicting "passion or two"; we will now turn our attention to the board.

••• THE ROLE OF DISTANCE •••

The use of space or the role of distance is another aspect of communication that is important to both preaching and theater. While the physical differences between a Broadway stage and a mainline pulpit may appear overwhelming, each manages to facilitate the same effect quite well. They create distance. They manage space. They enable discovery, illumination, pleasure, epiphany and—ultimately—encounter by making room for them.

Both theatre and preaching are events, occurrences—not things, but something happening. An agonistic, conflictual, motion-fraught event requires space. While the traditional pulpit is not everyone's idea of the optimal symbol of the relationship between the preacher and the congregation, and while it does not seem to provide for much in the way of physical movement, it does something essential. It provides distance.

The role of distance is first of all a practical one; the performer and the audience must be separated from each other in order for the audience to be able to see. Distance makes the sight lines work. This is not nothing. Many worship committees underestimate the importance of the congregation's being able to see (see chapter 6). But distance in the theatre or in the worship service provides for more than physical ease. It creates a place for something to happen. It creates arena.

The demarcated space becomes the servant of the performer (preacher or actor). It is the stuff that the performer has to work with. The process of a performer's manipulating his or her space is more readily observed in the theatre, certainly. One can see the phantom swoop or the heroine sweep across the boards, cutting a swath through the space with his presence or her energy. However, though large movement is not an option within the confines of the pulpit (and few preachers are skilled enough to handle large crosses back and forth through their chancels) the boundary the pulpit provides is as important to preaching as the perimeter of the arena or the proscenium arch are to the theatre. The pulpit focuses the congregation's attention on a common picture. As the performer carves the picture with her arms and hands, dimples it with his moues and grins, and perforates it with her fingers, the audience registers the three-dimensional experience as one body.

In this, the members of the congregation or audience feel their togetherness, and even, perhaps, make a kind of unconscious, corporate decision to withdraw to their own turf. In short, they help create the space for something to happen by taking up the role of listener. Psychologist James Hillman recognizes this kind of activity as a common characteristic of listening and labels it "negative capability." The principle is the same for audience as therapist: in order to make room for the other to become present, the listener must withdraw to a certain point.

> In the Jewish mystical doctrine of Tsimtsum, withdrawal is the essence of creativity. God the Creator, asserts Tsimtsum, is omnipotent and omnipresent, filling all space. In order for creation to occur, God must withdraw.... For the love of creation God withdraws.[17]

In this way, we may see what is perhaps the most important of the roles distance plays in theatre and preaching. Aesthetic distance creates psychological or spiritual space. The line of demarcation that separates the preacher and the congregation makes it possible for the person in the pew to have her own experience. Literal space makes figurative space possible.

The audience sits safely in the dark, and agrees to "suspend disbelief" (Coleridge). The congregation sits securely in its pews and opens their minds and hearts. They are vulnerable. The space makes it safe enough. Preachers have learned, as actors have, that "getting in somebody's face," "jumping down their throat," or violating their personal space is counterproductive.

Instead, like the artists of the theatre, preachers work to create a climate where the audience *may believe*. This ability to believe depends on getting the titrate just right—this much involvement, this much distance. Dramatist Oscar Brockett describes the desirable state as "semi-objectivity."

> The distance cannot be so great as to induce indifference...while a degree of detachment is necessary, involvement (empathy) is of equal importance.... Thus we watch a play with a double sense of concern and detachment. It is both a removed and an intensified reaction of a kind seldom possible outside esthetic experience.[18]

Psychological or spiritual experience requires a bit of space—not only in the colloquial sense of the word, but in the literal sense. This is something the theatre has always known.

Distance makes it possible for the audience to believe. Just as literal distance facilitates seeing, so psychological or spiritual distance facilitates belief. Why? Because belief is a kind of seeing.

The great American dramatist Thornton Wilder describes the phenomenon. He says that when we believe, we say, "This is the way things are. I have always known it without being fully aware that I knew it. Now in the presence of this play or novel or poem (or picture or piece of music) I know that I know it."[19] To believe, Wilder says, is to say "yes"—a kind of "grateful and self-forgetting acquiescence."[20] Specifically, the ability of theatre and preaching to show—to help us *see*—individual experience in terms of universal patterns, engenders belief. Again, as Wilder says, "It is through the theatre's power to raise the exhibited individual action into the realm of idea and type and universal that it is able to evoke our belief."[21] We believe because we recognize ourselves in the Story. Just as it is impossible for us to see something that is held up too closely to our eyes, so it is impossible for us to believe something pounded too forcefully into our minds and hearts. In both cases, apprehension breaks down because the key moment—the moment of recognition—is prevented.

Distance makes it possible, in theatre and in preaching, for the personal character of the relationship between performer and performee to be optimally "filtered." The alternative is an audience awash in a sea of pointless emotion. For preaching and theatre to work—for them to have integrity—distance has an important role to play. It is not that the relationship between performer and audience becomes impersonal, rather a certain amount of detachment makes it possible for the person in the pew to choose to close the gap (emotionally, psychologically, spiritually) between the preacher and himself or herself. It is this choice that constitutes the heart of the preaching moment. In this choice is the seed of belief.

✱✱✱ THE ROLE OF PERFORMANCE ✱✱✱

"Religion, like art, lives in so far as it is performed."[22] The notion of performance is the third bit of common ground that is crucial to both preaching and theatre. At minimum, performance involves the intentional presentation of self and implies the presence of others. We may perform our own words or those of someone else. We may perform Shakespeare or surgery or the duties of the Best Man. In performance, the self is an instrument for the following-through or carrying-out of an impulse. What is carried out may be an impulse to communicate, to accomplish a task or to execute a more involved process. When we embody or incarnate such an impulse, we are performing.

As Richard Ward reminds us, "The term performance comes from the old French *par* + *fournir*, which literally means to 'carry through to completion.' What is it that we do when we speak the sermon we have written in the study? Do we not bring it forth to completion in the act of speaking it?"[23]

It sounds simple and harmless enough. However, in practice preachers' feelings about "performing" are anything but. Of all the common territory that preachers and actors might share, this is the realm of the most distasteful stuff. This is the territory about which those of us who preach are likely to be most uncomfortable. This is the stuff that embarrasses us and that seems—somehow—out of sync with the gospel. Many preachers use the word "performance," in fact, as a way of designating inauthentic preaching—the very kind of preaching they themselves are trying to avoid.

The first problem with this negative attitude toward performance is that trying to avoid performance is a self-defeating enterprise. Once a preacher is in front of a congregation, she or he is performing. The only question is, is it better to be aware of, and therefore able to exercise some control over, the performance? This book takes the position that not only is it preferable that the preacher be aware of, and honest about, his or her self-presentation, but it is precisely in such awareness that we find the way to authentic preaching. Paradoxically, the key to authentic preaching is found in the notion of "honest performance."

The second problem with this negative view of performance is that it is shortsighted and ill-informed. A preacher presents himself or herself in a way that is quite similar to the way in which an actor presents himself or herself. Each hopes to serve a higher good: the playwright's vision, in the case of the actor; the Scripture text or its

Author, in the case of the preacher. The notion of "performance" or "self-presentation" does not necessarily imply that the self is being displayed for narcissistic or self-serving reasons (though it may be). Ideally, in the case of both theatre and preaching, performance means the use of self as vehicle—the disciplined giving of one's voice and body to a message, idea, or experience that needs one. Indeed, many artists have found such discipline to be a corrective for an inflated ego. And most seasoned preachers and observers of preachers find self-awareness and intentionality to be better predictors of a preacher's authenticity than performance energy or a taste for drama.

But a greater claim still may be made: performance is one of the preacher's most valuable exegetical tools. To be known, a text must be performed. (The same may be said to be true of the preacher's own sermon manuscript, although there are some obvious differences between the interpretive performance of one's own words and of the words of another.) "Expression deepens impression" as Leland Roloff has said. And it is peculiarly true of Scripture texts, so many of which began life in oral form, that the preacher or interpreter/performer can not be said to know the text until he or she has given it his or her voice and body. In the disciplined performing of the text, the text is made to live again. Early twentieth-century elocution teachers called it creating a quality of "first-timeness." Naturalness, accurate representation of spontaneous speech, and believability were required of the student before the quality was judged satisfactory.

More recently, Beverly Whitaker Long and Mary Francis Hopkins have begun to speak of literary texts as "arrested performances." Truly, if any texts deserve to be thought of as oral-aural events (oral performances) that just happen to be frozen in time by the convenient mechanism of print, biblical texts do. It is for this reason that we may say that the preaching moment begins not at 10:32 on Sunday morning as the preacher turns on the pulpit mike and announces "Hear the Word of God," but at four o'clock on Sunday afternoon, or at ten o'clock on Monday morning. The preaching moment begins in the study the minute the preacher picks up the Bible to speak aloud the text. For the preacher expression of the text, the performance or the giving of one's voice and body to a

49

text, starts the creative process and undergirds it throughout its course.

So Henri Bergson states:

> The performance of a work should not be thought of merely as an artistic accomplishment. Instead of coming at the end of one's studies, like an ornament, it should be at the beginning and throughout, as a support. Upon it we should place all the rest if we did not yield here and again to the illusion that the main thing is to discourse on things and that one knows them sufficiently when one knows how to talk **about** them.[24]

Too often, the preacher's interpretation of the text is a silent enterprise, as if all that can be known about the text can be known through the eyes. Too often, it is a sedentary exercise, as if all that is important about the text is what its linear, sequenced language component can tell us. Too often, the preacher is more anxious to know what the textual critic has to say about the text than to know what the voice of the text has to say.

It is not claimed here that everything that needs to be known about a text can be known by way of performance. What is claimed is:

1. It is appropriate for preaching's creative process to **start** the way the text itself started.
2. It is important for preaching's creative process to start the way it hopes to finish—with oral "life."
3. There are aspects—important aspects—of the meaning and the liveliness of the text that can only be known through speaking the words of the text aloud.

Thus, Charles Bartow says:

> Any serious attempt at homiletical inquiry must start with a concern for the spoken word as normative for the entire enterprise. From interpretation of Scripture to delivery of sermon based on it, the spoken word is typically an aural-oral, face-to-face event.... The "what" and the "how" of speech cannot be separated one from the other. They are perceived and responded to together.[25]

History is full of examples of artists who have known and depended upon this peculiar flow of creative energy between performance and text. W. B. Yeats, it is said, chanted his verse aloud as he wrote. "Seeking always the right word, which would convey his meaning and yet fit into the sound effect which he desired to create."[26] Others, like Herman Melville, apparently commandeered spousal support for a similar purpose. One imagines the author nightly settling a reluctant Mrs. Melville into the kitchen chair (there are apocryphal reports that he tied her in with a kitchen towel!) to hear the latest installment of his epic read aloud.

Robert Beloof tells of a young professor who discovered the significance of oral performance only after a miserable, public failure at poetry reading. Though he knew all there was to know about the poem and its author, the professor of literature missed interpreting the tone of the poem appropriately—or even approximately. After several weeks more of oral exploration, Beloof writes:

> He worked out a revealing reading. Puzzling over the reason why his critical labors had still left him short of a comprehension of tone, a comprehension which he achieved only after a further extensive exploration through voice and body, he said that perhaps it was like the differences between reading a map and trying to find one's way over the actual terrain.[27]

Beloof adds, "This is one of the most satisfying figures I have heard to describe the insights of those who have actually gone through the experience. For those who have not, it is, like love in the abstract, a very difficult thing to comprehend."[28]

For the preacher, the key to knowing the terrain as well as the map, is found in the notion of "honest performance." Actors call this quality "truthfulness." A performance, whether it is onstage or in the pulpit, is honest or truthful *when the interpreter is making careful use of experience.* An honest performance starts internally. The interpreter connects his or her experiences with the words of the text. The well-trained actor has many experiences to call upon (see chapter four). All of these—memories of emotions, sensory experiences, and visual stimuli, for example—feed the performance. However, in expressing the emotions, ideas, or events suggested by the text, the performer goes only as far as she or he can justify. That is, the expression of experience goes only as far as the experience.

The resulting communication is characterized by a degree of authenticity or sincerity that belies our stereotypic ideas about acting. Honest actors do not deceive. They show us something that is true. *They make themselves present in the words.* The more skilled and disciplined they are, the more accurately they show us ourselves. The more self-aware they are, the more deeply they reveal to us the nature of humankind.

Make no mistake. The kind of interpretation and performance we have been talking about is neither hysterical or flaky, histrionic or uncontrolled. To say that a process makes use of experience is not the same thing as saying that it is undisciplined. Performance is an art form that makes disciplined, practical use of experience and imagination. Well-trained performers are the "Irish policemen" of the artistic realm, it is said. They dream with both feet planted firmly on the ground.

In the performance of Scripture, the preacher gives his or her body and voice to the text for the purpose of bringing it to life in a particular context. All the preacher's physical, mental, and spiritual skills (see chapter 3) are brought to bear in the task of interpreting and embodying the text. When all goes well, a bodily entelechy is achieved which, as it is blessed by the Holy Spirit, may allow those who have ears to hear. When all goes ideally, the preacher and congregation are caught up in a creative process that has the power to transform both sides of the chancel.

We have identified action, distance, and performance as ingredients that are crucial in this preaching and theatre. While they do not account for all of what constitutes the arts, they represent some of their most important aspects. They also suggest that territory that the arts of preaching and theatre hold in common is of a certain size and depth. Although preaching and theatre have still more in common than has been suggested here, we will content ourselves with one more way of making the comparison.

✦✦✦ THE CREATIVE PROCESS ✦✦✦

As we have said, in the comparison of theatre and preaching, a certain similarity of vocabulary is obvious. It is striking to note that preachers, uncomfortable as they may be with other trappings of the theatre, show an affinity for its language. It is more startling still to hear secular actors use language that carries religious overtones. Sometimes in articulating their experience with interpreting and embodying texts, actors use religious vocabulary outright. Jerzy Growtowski's notion of the "holy" actor or Richard Boleslavsky's interest in harnessing the actor's "spiritual forces"[29] are examples.

In her seminal book, *The Word's Body: An Incarnational Aesthetic of Interpretation*, Alla Bozarth-Campbell describes the creative process using the theological categories of Creation, Incarnation, and Transformation. The labels are suggestive for both preachers and actors. The task of the first phase of the process—that of Creation—might be understood as that of hearing the voice of the text. "In the beginning God said..." "In the beginning was the Word..." In the beginning of the performance process it is the task of the actor or the preacher to *hear* what the text is saying. The performer's work in this stage is disciplined by what actors call "stripping," the setting aside of one's idiosyncrasies, expectations, and habitual attitudes. For the preacher the work of this phase of the process may well be understood in kenotic, or self-empty-ing, terms. But the central task is the same. Both are seeking to enter the creative process by hearing a word, a word that comes from outside the performing self. Creativity starts for the preacher and the actor with lis-tening.

Incarnation is the phase where two separate entities join to cre-ate a third entity *in which the integrity of each is still preserved.*[30] An actor joins the script, a preacher joins the text, and a third thing is born of the union. The third thing has still absolutely the essen-tial properties of its parents. The actor's arms, the preacher's face, they are still the actor's arms and the preacher's face. But they are enmeshed now in the something-happening of the play or the ser-mon. "The dancer is the dance," as they say.

Actors find it useful in this phase to work linking word and body. They move as they seek to connect with the play's dramatic action or "spine." Speech flows and the director may even allow the actors to "roam." Discoveries and decisions made in this way have "the advan-tage of having been born in action."[31] Sermons too that come out of pacing, roaming, or even driving are likely to have an advantage.

The third phase, Transformation, flows naturally from the second.

53

As the preacher is caught up in the sermon, the preacher is changed. As the hearers are caught up in the play or the preaching, they give something of themselves to it and they accept some of it into themselves—and they are changed. The transforming process for the preacher and the actor and their audiences is one of gap-filling.

The transformative aspect of the creative process clearly applies both to the performer and the audience and is present in both the Creation and Incarnation phases of the creative process as well. However, in order to get a feel for the gap-filling that is characteristic of this stage of the process, let us focus on the experience of the members of the audience or congregation during the transformation phase.

1. The members of audience or congregation may be assumed to have entered in to the something-happening or the unfolding of the sermon. They have not only been caught up in the sermons's momentum, but have felt drawn or repulsed, motivated or alienated or some other such movement of their own. (ACTION)
2. We may also assume that the audience or congregation has been allowed the optimal blend of detachment and involvement so that the question of how to respond to the sermon or play is truly a matter of choice. (DISTANCE)
3. Finally, we may imagine that the performer's honest expression of the text has unleashed its life and its power, opening it and making it accessible to the audience member. (PERFORMANCE)

What happens then, or what may happen, is that the audience member chooses to close one or more of the gaps that have been left to him. He may, for example, decide to do the work of drawing a mental picture of one of the text's images on his internal motion picture screen. Or she may choose to like the performer. Someone else may attach the memories of a painful personal experience to a story the performer tells, amplifying it for herself. Whenever audience members do one of these things or something like one of these things, whenever they fill in or add to or affirm or amplify, they open themselves up to change. In doing the "work" that the performance has offered them, they invest themselves and so make themselves more open to being changed. Artists refer to this aspect of the process as "filling the gaps."

When these various phases and aspects of the creative process are arranged in what might be their chronological form, a certain resonance between theological and aesthetic concerns may also be seen. It is important to remember, however, that any attempt to chronologize the creative process, though helpful as a heuristic device, is misleading. The creative process is organic, not mechanical. It moves in circular and not altogether predictable lines, the so-called "phases" bleeding one into another.

ASPECTS OF THE CREATIVE PROCESS

theological category	preacher's concerns	actor's concerns	practical implications for preachers
CREATION "In the beginning, God said..."	the text's voice ◆◆◆ kenotic	the text's voice ◆◆◆ stripping	read the text aloud throughout process
INCARNATION "The Word became flesh..."	embodying sermon's action ◆◆◆ skinotic	embodying dramatic action ◆◆◆ spine	words should be born in action
TRANSFORMATION "As the Spirit gave them utterance"	connecting with the congregation ◆◆◆ plurotic	connecting with other actors ◆◆◆ space, seeing, spontaneity	leave gaps

✦✦✦ CONCLUSION ✦✦✦

In examining the intersection between preaching and theatre, we have discovered a great deal of common ground. Preaching and theatre share at least three characteristics, a creative process, and a rootedness in art. Three key characteristics and their potential benefits were noted: action, which enables encounter; distance, which facilitates belief; and performance, which releases power. We began to sketch the practical implications of the theatre's kinship with preaching. The following two chapters will continue that tack.

Chapter Three

Basic Training for Performance

Nothing is more important in sermon performance than the voice—not the face, not the arms, not the hands. As important as gestures and facial expressions are, the role they play in the preaching moment is a supporting one. While it is true that in most public speaking settings, nonverbal communication—the communication achieved by the face, body, and vocal tone—is stronger than the sheer force of the words themselves, in much preaching the power of voice is stronger still. It is the preacher's voice, comprised of thought, emotion, instinctive impulse, sensory response, and vocal/physical action, that sets the stage for the sermon. In many cases, it not only sets the stage but builds the sets and brings in the props as well, so important is its role.

Noted speech communication theorist Albert Mehrabian has shown that 55 percent of all meaning communicated in a face-to-face setting is communicated by the body, 38 percent by the tone of voice, and only 7 percent by the actual words spoken. This explains nicely what we already know: if a speaker's verbal and nonverbal communications contradict each other, it is the nonverbal that will be believed. However, in much preaching, Mehrabian's formula skews decidedly toward the verbal/vocal elements of the act since much of the preacher's body is likely to be "unavailable" to the congregation. Hidden behind the wooden walls of a tall pulpit, perhaps, or a Geneva gown, the preacher's body is largely unseen. Often, what is not hidden is obscured by distance. The preacher's face, for example, is easily read only by those in the first few pews. Distance, blocking, costuming, and often poor sight lines mean that members of the congregation must rely more heavily on their ears.[2]

[Not only is the voice the preacher's most powerful tool, it is his or her most personal. Nothing conveys more about the personality of the preacher.] Admittedly, our bodies are capable of communicating a great deal. Freud put it dramatically, "A man cannot lie. If he lies with his lips he will chatter the truth from his fingertips." However, in the pulpit, what we say with our face and gesture does not reveal what our voices reveal. This is especially true in regard to self-revelation. Our voices reveal more about us than any other single aspect of our communication style. Why? Because voices are made of breath. There is nothing more intimately ours—more interior to us—than our voices. There is no more sensitive way to "outer" our inner thoughts and feelings than with our voices.

One of my ground rules for introductory classes in preaching is that while most kinds of peer feedback are encouraged, only the instructor may critique vocal mannerisms. I carefully explain the reasons for this rule to each entering class. One is that vocal problems are often obvious and sometimes distracting. I want the class to get beyond their first set of impressions and ask themselves some deeper questions about the effectiveness of the sermon. The other is that many students find it difficult to hear their voice evaluated. Some people, in fact, would rather have their face evaluated than their voice. A careful approach is required. Even students whose self-esteem can easily withstand a tough review written in red pen at the end of a term paper, sometimes find themselves feeling defensive during vocal coaching. They may feel that it is they themselves—even their very souls—that are being given critique.

It is precisely because of the personal quality of the voice that vocal work provides the preacher with a valuable way of knowing. Reading the biblical text aloud helps a trained reader bring to consciousness his or her own biases, affinities, and associations. Such material is grist for the interpreter's mill. Its use enriches the reader's understanding of the text. In addition, a disciplined, sensitive reading of a text—a reading that is informed and guided by the kinds of principles and disciplines outlined in this chapter—may reveal something of the writer's heart and mind. Through such experiences as reproducing the text's rhythms, word colors, and "mouth feel" and through the kinesthetic experience of linking the reader's breath and the writer's phrase, a process of identification is set up. The reader aligns his or her voice with the writer's and finds out something about the author's mind and heart that could not be discovered in any other way.

So intimate is the connection between emotional experience and vocal production that some specialists have found therapeutic value in voice work. The underlying assumption of such work is that the voice not only reveals emotion but "remembers" it, especially in the case of traumatic experience.

> If the breath is affected and altered by even a quiver of emotion (the remembrance of a sad or funny event, a slight shock like a near miss, or a gasp of recognition when we suddenly meet an old friend) as it always is, then it must follow that more powerful violations...will penetrate deep into the breathing mechanism and lodge there...until eradicated.[3]

In such cases, release or purging may be possible through the use of relaxation and deep-breathing exercises.

Certainly, if we believe that muscles and nerves "remember" trauma, as in some cases of phantom pain or functional arthritis, for example, it is not difficult to believe that the breathing apparatus would have such a capacity. And although most breathing habits result from superficial causes, the insight of vocal therapists is a valuable one; the connection between breath and emotion is not to be underestimated. Regardless of whether we are talking about psychic trauma or the lightest of human emotions, the voice is one of the preacher's most sensitive instruments—not only for expressing but for knowing.

Most of us take our voices as much for granted as we do our breath. (*More* for granted if you consider that we think at least occasionally about our breath, after a run, for example, or when someone is passing around peppermints.) We tend to treat our voices as if they operated on automatic pilot or as if they were controlled by an unconscious mechanism as respiration is. Some even make the assumption that each person's voice is a given and should not be tampered with.

A man who tries to make a change in the way he uses his voice, for example by finding its natural pitch range, may be regarded with suspicion. A woman who makes an effort to learn to project her voice may find that not everyone is enthusiastic. Sometimes undisciplined voices or voices that are a great deal less effective than they could be are excused by the thinking, "That's just me" or "At least I'm not putting on airs." To most listeners it is more important that a speaker be natural than almost anything else. Many people are surprised to learn that being natural and being effective are not mutually exclusive goals.

It may be that the average church member has good reason to mistrust the sound of a trained voice. Pulpit tones, golden throats, and preachers who are in love with the sound of their own voices are not legendary for no reason. A trained voice is often associated with condescension or pretension. However, for most of us, our most effective physical instrument is not the one that comes to us automatically. Most voices need tending. There is no voice that does not need attention. Every voice can profit from exercise.

There is no reason to believe that tending to the voice, i.e., by building its strength, freedom, and flexibility, will result in a phonier you, despite the common fear. The goal of vocal work, in fact, is quite the opposite: to uncover the best you, the most natural you. The most important vocal work a preacher can do is the work of freeing his or her voice, that is, the work of sifting out what is effective and authentic from the habits that have built up over the course of a lifetime.

Freeing the human voice to be an effective instrument of expression is a task that requires effort, guidance, and experimentation. Although each of us has a natural voice—a voice that is uniquely ours and is uniquely effective—few of us uncover this voice without expending some effort. Few of us begin our speaking careers with a voice that will last the length of that career. Few of us set out on the journey to becoming a preacher knowing everything we need to know about the voice God gave us.

Most of us start with several abilities and skills in place. Some of us have an ear for emphasis and seem to know instinctively which word to stress in order to make the meaning plain. Some seem to come from the womb equipped with FM radio voices. Others have an ability for which they cannot account logically and which enables them to orchestrate the pace and timing of their speaking so as to keep the listeners on the edge of their seats. All of these, undergirded by the discipline of concentration, play an important role in the use of the voice to interpret texts. But no one is enough in itself.

Developing the voice for the purposes of interpreting the text (whether *text* is defined as Scripture to be read aloud in worship or a sermon manuscript to be delivered) is a bit like ballet dancers "taking class." It represents an ongoing, even a daily, commitment to both physical and interpretive disciplines. The voice, like a dancer's body, is an instrument that needs nurturing and stretching. To reach its full potential, it must be explored and experimented with.

••• Exploring the Physical Voice •••

Vocal production is first of all a function of breath support. Just as a dancer relearns such fundamental abilities as standing and walking, so the speaker must relearn what is perhaps the most fundamental of all human habits—breathing. While the breathing habits that one uses automatically in daily life are sufficient for many communication tasks, they are not sufficient for public speaking. Public speaking requires a degree of vocal projection and breath duration that is not necessary in conversational speech. In addition, it is common for public speaking to enlarge and exacerbate the small habits that are relatively harmless in conversational speech. A vocal production glitch magnified—that is, produced louder and sustained longer—is not only more noticeable but more likely to result in damage to the vocal mechanism.

In order to provide the longer, more powerful breaths upon which a healthy preaching voice is built, it is necessary to shift the focus of breathing. Untrained speakers are likely to think first of the lungs and rib cage. The problem with focusing attention there is that the actual physical movement that occurs in such breathing is likely to occur in the area of the collar bone. It is the collar bone that rises and falls as the lungs take in air. Breathing that is not adjusted to the needs of the public speaking setting is relatively shallow, involving the upper portion of the lungs and unnecessarily tense, focusing muscle tension at or near the site of the vocal folds.

Deep breathing, also referred to as diaphragmatic breathing, is the kind of breathing that undergirds an effective preaching voice. It focuses on the area an inch or two below the belt buckle. The diaphragm, the large shelf-like muscle that forms a wall between the chest cavity and the abdominal cavity, helps control the flow of breath. Diaphragmatic breathing makes longer, more powerful breaths possible while at the same time shifting the focus of movement and muscle tension away from the area of the throat. This kind of deep breathing, the same kind practiced by trained singers, results not only in sustainable, powerful breath support but in a freer voice—a voice less affected by excess tension.

To begin the shift from clavicular breathing to diaphragmatic breathing, many people find it helpful to lie down. When one lies supine on the floor or other firm surface, diaphragmatic breathing is automatic. The abdominal muscles that are located adjacent to the diaphragm relax and contract so that the abdomen rises and falls with the breath. Inspiration results in what looks like a filling of the abdominal cavity with air. Exhalation appears to deflate the abdomen.

What is really happening, of course, is a bit different. It is simple, if not observable to the naked eye. Since the diaphragm cannot be controlled directly, the speaker is dependent upon the abdominal muscles to control its movement. When the abdominal muscles relax (pooching out the midriff area), the diaphragm tightens and flattens, allowing the lungs to fill up with air. When the abdominal muscles contract (flattening or drawing in the abdominal area) the diaphragm expands up in a dome-shaped position, pushing against the bottom of the lungs, helping to expel the air. Lying on one's back helps to neutralize the muscles that normally control the rise and fall of the rib cage—the muscles one is tempted to rely on when standing. When a person is relaxed in the supine position, these muscles are less likely to try to get into the act. The more powerful, advantageously located abdominal muscles are freed to take over. As the stress-point of vocal production moves south, so does the pinched voice problem that plagues so many preachers.

Deeper breathing helps to produce not only more powerful voices and freer, more natural voices but sometimes freer, more natural speakers. Typically, this happens after the shift to diaphragmatic breathing has become second nature. The rewards of developing the physical voice can be rich indeed. Much more than a louder voice is at stake. It may be that in doing the hard work required to build and free our physical voices, we will find out something about our spiritual voices as well.

> Ideally, voice work should feed organically into...plain speaking without conscious application of technique. If the work to free the voice has been deeply absorbed, the person will be naturally freer; the person and the voice will be unified.... The aim is not just a well-tuned instrument but a continuously reopened road leading into and out of the creative center.[4]

✦✦✦ EXPERIMENTING WITH RESONANCE ✦✦✦

Singers speak of three kinds of voices: three areas of the body where the voice may be reinforced, amplified, and colored. In effect, these areas act as a concert band shell or as the body of a cello does to reinforce sound. Without such cavities the human body's ability to produce a receivable sound would be quite limited. Breath support on its own has little "broadcast" power.

"Head" voice is voice that is focused in the upper chambers of the vocal mechanism and is often used in singing higher pitches. Sometimes it has a kind of falsetto quality; sometimes it might be described simply as a light, clear vocal quality. The "middle" voice is focused in the middle chambers of the vocal mechanism. It is often used with the middle pitch range and may have a rounder, fuller sound. Finally, what some singers refer to as the "chest" voice is focused in the lower chambers of the vocal apparatus. Often, this voice is used to color lower pitched tones. It is called a "chest" voice because it seems to result partly from vibrations around the lower throat, upper chest, and collarbone.

These three types of voices have provided generations of singers and speakers with a helpful way of organizing their thinking about resonance. However, it is important to note that the designations "head," "middle," and "chest" are more heuristic devices than literal descriptions. Actual resonance is achieved mostly in the nose, mouth, and throat.[5]

Nasal resonance is easy to recognize. Most people can readily imitate both hypo-nasality and hyper-nasality. Hypo-nasality is the sound of a stopped-up nose: "I'b got uh co'd id my nod." Hyper-nasality is the sound of a well-known switchboard operator: "One ringy-dingy." Placing the fingers on the bridge of the nose, keeping the mouth closed, and running through the sounds *mmmm, nnnn,* and *ng* will provide an excellent example of nasal resonance. Unfortunately, a speaker's ability to control nasal resonance is limited. While increased awareness may enhance these nasal sounds, balanced nasality is largely a function of healthy nasal passages.

A colorful exception to this rule is the related problem of assimilative nasality. There is plenty that can be done to change this habit. Try the sentence "Amanda and Dan were fond of meandering in the garden." Do the *a*'s sound pinched? tight? squeezed? Like a Brooklyn accent? You may have assimilative nasality, a condition where the soft palate at the back of the mouth lowers into position for the *m* in *Amanda* and then lazily stays there for the following *a*—or where the soft palate anticipates the *n* in *Dan* and so slops over a nasal sound into the *a*. In both cases, the nasal sound "contaminates" an adjacent sound, resulting in a particularly unpleasant hybrid.

The remedy for assimilative nasality is increased awareness and control of the soft palate plus attentiveness to the resulting sound. Clear vowel sounds are the goal. The position and rise of the palate may be observed in the course of a yawn. The soft palate is identifiable as the portion of the mouth that is in front of the uvula and is raised in the middle of a yawn. A lowered soft palate admits air into the nasal cavities to reinforce sounds. The most common cause of excessive nasality is this palate's "laziness" or slowness to rise.

If you are struggling with excessive nasality in a case where the nasal consonant precedes the vowel, try extending the consonant to give the soft palate a bit of extra time to raise. For example, in the word *man*, practice lengthening the *m* to two or three times its normal length before pronouncing the *a*. Repeat the word, gradually shortening the *m* to its normal length. In the case where the vowel precedes the nasal consonant, such as in the word *am*, try focusing on the mouth movement necessary to produce the vowel. Lengthen the sound and exaggerate the movement until, gradually, you are able to produce a "clean" *a* of normal duration.

What singers call the "chest" voice is mostly comprised of throat, especially lower-throat resonance. Since the throat or pharynx is the largest resonance cavity, it is best suited to reinforcing the voice's lower pitch tones. In order for the throat to provide optimal resonance, the speaker must be relaxed. Relaxation, important in the use of all three resonance chambers, is crucial for the use of the lower throat. The tissues of the pharynx are relatively soft, tending to dampen out the higher pitched tones and nicely color the lower ones. When the walls of the throat are affected by excessive tension, however, they become hardened, reinforcing the higher pitches and doing nothing for the lower.

Therefore, diaphragmatic breathing is the most important ingredient of pharyngeal resonance. In addition to the relaxation process outlined at the end of this chapter, the preacher may want to focus extra attention on the relaxation of the arm. Tensing the hands and biceps and releasing that tension results in a sensation of relaxation in the throat. Relaxation of the tongue is also important for chest resonance. A sustained *ah* should produce a tongue that is only slightly elevated (check it with a mirror if you are not sure; you should be able to see the top of the throat) and an open, wide passage connecting the mouth and the throat. Narrowing this key passageway may substantially reduce pharyngeal resonance.

Oral resonance, or what singers call the "middle" voice, is the easiest of the resonance cavities to control. Its size and shape can be modified by appropriate articulation. Quick improvement is observable in speakers who simply focus attention on lip and tongue activity. A slight exaggeration, or even just an increased consciousness of lip and tongue movement, seem to result almost automatically in the "forward placement" of vocal tones. For the purposes of public speaking, a general emphasis on forward placement is helpful. Retracted sounds, sounds that are focused near the back of the mouth, are difficult to project. Sounds brought well forward in the mouth tend to be crisper, cleaner, and more free.

Placement is largely a result of the movement and shaping of the tongue but is also affected by the dropping and closing of the jaw, which creates vertical space, and the position of the lips, which control the shape of the opening. The placement of vowel sounds is an especially important aspect of oral resonance and will be reviewed briefly here. Text books on phonetics and speech pathology that provide a more detailed description of the workings of oral resonance are widely available.[6]

There are at least ten separate places in the oral cavity where vowels are formed. We will focus on six of the most useful sites. The four "corners" of the oral cavity produce:

1. Focused at the extreme top/front of the oral cavity is the long *ee* sound, symbolized in the phonetic alphabet as *(i)* and found in such words as *see, knee, free.*
2. The top/back corner of the mouth produces the long *u* sound, symbolized as *(u)* and found in such words as *true, new,* and *whose.*
3. The lower/back of the oral cavity produces the short *o* sound, symbolized as *(a)* and found in words like *God, harm* and *honest.*
4. The lower/front of the mouth produces the short *a* sound, symbolized as *(ae)* and found in such words as *can't, laugh* and *half.*
5. The middle of the mouth is used chiefly for producing the *uh* and *er* sounds found in such words as *sofa* and *earn.*
6. The short *i* sound *(sit)*, the long *a* sound *(play)* and the short *e* sound *(end)*, are all focused at the front of the mouth.

The sounds that must be placed at the extreme front of the mouth include, in "descending" order, that is, from the top of the mouth to the bottom: long *e,* short *i,* long *a,* short *e,* and short *a.* Try the sentence, "See him make friends laugh," and you should be able to feel the progression of the vowels' placement from the top/front of the mouth to the lower/front. Remember, this is not an exercise in pitch, but placement. You are paying attention to the precise physical location of the sound. Try to sense where it is focused.

If this seems difficult at first, start with the extremes. Practice going from the long *ee* sound *(seek)* to the short *o* sound *(God).* Notice that *seek* seems to happen high on the roof of your mouth and all the way forward at a site just behind your upper front teeth. *God* seems to focus in the opposite corner, all the way in the back of the mouth and the bottom of the cavity.

Try the following sentences, charting the placement of the vowel sounds as you go. Some of these are veritable dances—the resonance seeming to ricochet from one key point in the mouth to another. Savor the sensations. Play with the sounds. Let your palate tingle and your tongue cavort.

1. Hear, O Israel.
   The movement is from the extreme upper-front *(hear)* to the middle-back *(O)* and back to a glissando of vowel sounds, descending across the front of the mouth *(Israel).*
2. Thus says the Lord.
   The movement is a gentle cha-cha: starting from the middle of the mouth *(thus)* forward to the mid-front *(says)* back to the middle *(the)* and one step farther back *(Lord).*
3. Taste and see that the Lord is good.
   The movement is almost a box-step: from upper-front *(taste)* to extreme upper-front *(see)* to mid-back *(Lord)* to upper-back *(good).*
4. The sea flows, the wind howls.
   The movement of the two phrases is two nearly parallel slides in the mouth; from extreme upper-front *(sea)* to mid-back *(flows)* and from a slightly lower upper-front *(wind)* to a slightly lower mid-back *(howls).*

5. Our help is in the name of the Lord.

The movement begins in the mid-back *(our)*, bounces forward *(help, is, in, name)* and moves through the middle *(of, the)* and to the back *(Lord)*.

••• EXPERIMENTING WITH ARTICULATION •••

Technically, the word *articulation* applies to the production of consonants, and the word *enunciation* applies to the production of vowels. However, the distinction is a bit arcane and for our purposes it will do to lump the question of all speech sounds into the category of articulation. (Though, of course, we have already shown that much of what is important about the production of vowel sounds has to do with placement and resonance.) We might also use the word *diction*; it is, after all, the word most people use to refer to the shaping of speech sounds. However, since *diction* may also indicate the selection of words in a linguistic system, let us agree on *articulation* as the word that best captures the issue of precision and clarity in the forming of phonemes, or speech sounds.

Articulation may be defined as the process by which the air stream is modified for the production of speech sounds. These modifications result from the activity of agents that are sometimes known as "the articulators": the teeth, tongue, lips, palate, and jaw. We might also include the larynx in our list of articulators. It certainly has its role to play in the modification of the breath stream. The laryngeal mechanism does much of the work of adjusting the vocal bands' tension, for example. However, for practical purposes, let us focus on those agents that carve up the air stream in a way that is readily observable: the lips, tongue, and palate.

Consonants that are formed by the lips, called *labials*, fall roughly into two groups. One group is the flip-side of the other. The sound *p* and the sound *b* are made at the same site. One belongs to the voiced group of consonants that have resonance *(b)*, the other to the voiceless group of consonants that are all breath *(p)*. The sounds *v/f* and *w/wh* have similar relationships. In addition, *m* may be considered a labial. Though most of what it takes to make an *m* sound happens in the nasal cavities, the lips are needed to shape the sound.

Voiceless and nasal sounds are the white under-belly of the world of articulation. When speakers begin to attend to their articulation, they almost always begin with the voiced consonants. Often they end up with a speech package that features popping hard consonants (*b, v, d, z,* and *w,* for example) and fading everything else. Most people who have even a small amount of public speaking experience (they've taught a Sunday school class or given a presentation to a small group of coworkers) should focus their articulation energy on the more-often-neglected voiceless and nasal consonants. They present the speaker with a less-obvious target and provide a bit more challenge; but if a speaker can perfect their use, the voiced consonants will often come along (more or less automatically) for the ride.

Pronounce the following sentences, paying particular attention to the articulator indicated.

> 1. Voiceless and nasal consonants
>   LIPS :   Whip up some muffins on a whim.
>   TONGUE: Thin, tan rats run last.
>   PALATE: King Kong can climb.
>
> 2. Voiced consonants
>   LIPS: Believe vows.
>   TONGUE: Does the raja doze?
>   PALATE: Going, going, gone.
>
> 3. Voiced and voiceless consonants together
>   LIPS: I know whom I have believed.
>   TONGUE: Delight thy heart in the Lord.
>   PALATE: Go get the king.

It may be helpful at this point to note a rule of thumb for pronouncing words that contain both voiced and voiceless consonants. While this rule is hardly important in everyday conversation, it becomes important in the amplified or projected speech required in public speaking settings.

69

RULE: When a voiced consonant is followed immediately by a voiceless consonant, the voiceless consonant becomes voiced.

EXAMPLES: *God's* is pronounced *Godz.*
Words is pronounced *Wordz.*
Deeds is pronounced *Deedz.*

••• COMMON PROBLEMS WITH THE VOICE •••

The following list of vocal problems is meant to represent the areas of difficulty most often encountered by those who read Scripture and preach. A brief remedy is suggested for each. A wider discussion may be found in any number of speech texts.[7] For persistent problems, work with a speech therapist may be indicated.

1. INDISTINCT CONSONANTS

Perhaps the most common problem with vocal production in the public speaking setting is garbled or indistinct consonants. "Sloppy diction" is what this condition would be called in common parlance. Sounds that are mushy when they should be hard or crisp may indicate shyness, uncertainty, laziness, or passive resistance in a speaker. An exaggeration of lip, tongue, teeth, and jaw movement is often enough to effect a quick cure. For many, however, producing precise sounds is not the only difficulty. Psychological and physical projection are also important for the production of sounds that "read" or carry to the back pew.

2. MOUTH-AS-SLIT

Interestingly, this condition seems to occur most often in mustached and bearded men. However, it is far from uncommon in the hairless. More than half of the untrained speakers I encounter could benefit from dropping the jaw. Perhaps as many as 25 percent of these have a serious problem. A mouth that is opened too narrowly produces garbled sounds: retracted vowels and sluggish consonants. Moreover, the projection that is necessary for public speaking is rendered exceedingly difficult. The antidote for this condition is to practice speaking vowel sounds with enough distance between the top and bottom teeth so that two fingers can be inserted in that space.

3. RETRACTED VOICE

In some speakers more than the occasional vowel sound is retracted—the whole voice seems to lodge in or near the top of the throat. The point where placement, resonance, and articulation happen in the mouth is significantly farther back than is effective. Cockney and Valley Girl dialects are examples of the retracted voice. Typically, it is a dulled and hollowed sound, where sounds that should be pronounced well forward in the oral cavity are "swallowed" instead.

Exaggerated facial movement (tongue, jaw, but especially the lips) can neatly cure this condition if the speaker is willing. It is also possible to "think" the sounds forward in the mouth. Try practicing speaking with the jaw dropped and the face tilted downward toward the floor, imagining that gravity is helping to pull the sounds forward in the mouth.

4. EXCESSIVE GLOTTAL TENSION

It is easy to train the ear to spot "tight" speakers. Though their voices are typically pinched, sounding sometimes strident or even thin, there is a simple test to diagnose the problem: when one imagines reproducing the sounds of a tight speaker, the glottis automatically tightens vocal response to the point of discomfort. Excessive vocal tension is caused by allowing muscle tension to creep into the glottal area.

Such tension may travel from surrounding areas or as a result of the speaker's conscious effort to "gear up" for projection. For some speakers it seems to be a result of the natural nervousness that accompanies public speaking. Converting such energy to "race horse" energy, practicing relaxation and diaphragmatic breathing, provides some relief. There are also those who swear by more psychological techniques—such as imaging a large, warm grapefruit at the back of the mouth. Swallowing is also a quick but very short-range cure for excessive tension. It is especially important that the swallow be a gentle one. Hard swallowing and throat clearing do more harm than good.

5. NASALITY

As has been explained, hyper-nasality often results from a slow or "lazy" palate. The delayed movement of the palate allows extra air—more air than is optimal—up into the nasal passages. The obvious treatment is to retrain the palate to move more quickly to block the flow of air into the nasal cavity. In addition, it will be important to balance out hyper-nasality. To accomplish this, the speaker must look for ways to add more oral and "chest" resonance. A tried-and-true measure that is effective in treating both of these problems involves the dropping of the jaw and the forward placement of sounds in the mouth.

6. TEETH-TONGUE LISP

Hissy s sounds often result from an imperfect meeting of the teeth. When the top-front and the bottom-front teeth do not approximate—come together in the ideal nearly touching pattern—excessive sibilance results. Since most people have imperfect mouths, most people have some problem with sibilance. Such a problem may be especially annoying when the speaker is working with a microphone, since microphones seem to like to join in the fun of distorting s sounds.

To compensate for and minimize this problem, the speaker must experiment with finding the best s sound for himself or herself. The lower jaw must come forward and the teeth must approximate. The sides of the tongue must always be at the upper molars. The tip of the tongue is positioned either at the gum ridge above the upper teeth (pointing slightly downward) or behind the lower teeth. The goal is to discover the way the speaker can achieve a focused air stream—an air stream with the least amount of excess air as possible. Try making the sound *t* as in the word *take*. Say the word and then let your teeth return to the *t* position. Now, without moving your teeth, say *steak*. The best *s* you can make will come from a carefully focused air stream produced while your mouth is in this *t* position.

7. FADING VOLUME

One of the most common complaints of listeners is that the speaker trails off at the ends of sentences. Whole words are lost. Listeners are frustrated. Fading volume is often a result of insufficient breath support. The speaker should not be told to try harder or to talk louder. The only effective treatment for this common and maddening problem is for the speaker to retrain his or her breathing. Diaphragmatic breathing and a desire to project or connect are requisite for speaking so that 100 percent of what is said can be heard in the back pew.

✦✦✦ PREPARING THE BODY ✦✦✦

Much of the body work necessary for preaching has been covered already in the description and exercises concerned with diaphragmatic breathing. The key to physical preparation for preaching is found in this practice and in the related disciplines of relaxation and flexibility. The great acting teacher Constantin Stanislavski, originator of what became the Method school of acting, believed that muscle tension interfered with inner emotional experience.[8] He proved the importance of muscle relaxation by asking actors to hold up the end of a grand piano while multiplying 37 times 9 in their heads, or recounting the shop fronts in the two blocks before the theatre or singing an aria. The actors discovered that it was necessary to set the piano down and take time to relax their muscles before they were able to perform such tasks. Muscle relaxation is important to a preacher's creative process in a similar way. Flexibility is also cultivated in preaching in order to create a physical instrument that is responsive to the finest of the preacher's emotions. A wider examination of these disciplines and a suggested routine for incorporating them into daily life follow.

In addition to the relaxation exercises associated with breathing, the preacher must also give time and attention to exercises that increase muscle length and flexibility. While basic training to increase diaphragmatic breathing may be learned in a few months and require only occasional exercises after the initial period of adjustment, there is no end to the stretching of muscles. Every preacher should perform simple stretching exercises every day.

The target of such exercises includes the large muscles of the legs and arms and such key muscles as those of the neck and lower back. The aim of such exercises is to achieve and maintain a *responsive* body. Preaching's nonverbal aspects require a body that is ready to express the widest possible range of ideas and feelings, from the most subtly nuanced theological thought to the largest of human emotions. Preachers deal on a cosmic scale; their bodies must be up to the scope of the task. At the same time, preachers deal on a finely calibrated scale; their bodies must be up to the precision such a task requires.

The fact that preachers must overcome such obstacles as sight-line problems and Geneva gowns in order to make their nonverbal communication available to the congregation does not excuse them from developing a flexible, responsive body. A trained body is more likely to find a way to express itself despite such obstacles, and the potential power of such expression is huge. Basic training for the preacher's body focuses on one essential exercise and may be supplemented by others as needed.

THE ROLL-DOWN[9]

The exercise begins standing, weight balanced equally on feet shoulders' width apart. The arms hang easily at the sides, hands relaxed. A straight, but not rigid, spine shapes the posture. A fishing line may be envisioned to be hooked through the front middle of the collar bone, lifting the body slightly. The shoulders fall back naturally without being forced.

- After establishing the base position described above, **begin a gentle neck roll.** Take care not to let the shoulders rise in response to the head movement. Get a long, slow stretch of the neck muscles. Side and front stretches should be pushed gradually to increase the range of the stretch. However, caution should be exercised with the backward stretch; a gentler touch is required in this case.

- When the neck is relaxed, **drop the head** so the top or crown of the head is parallel with the floor. **Let the top of the head lead you toward the floor,** rolling the torso forward very slowly. It is important to picture in the mind's eye a vertebrae by vertebrae progression. (When the exercise is done with a partner, one partner "spots" while the other executes the exercise. The spotter touches the partner's spine lightly, moving slowly down the back, pointing out with the touch each vertebrae, helping the partner keep the movement slow and smooth.) Care should be taken to insure that the top of the head stays parallel to the floor as the torso is lowered and that the knees are never locked.
- During the course of the roll-down, the arms will swing forward naturally. **When the lowest comfortable point is reached, extend the arms forward** as if stretching for an object just out of reach. **Relax the arms and repeat.** By tensing and releasing the tension of the extended arm, additional back muscles may be involved in the relaxation exercise.
- When the head and torso are lowered to the farthest comfortable point, **shake the hands vigorously,** one at a time, to release their tension. (It is also possible to "shake out the face" in a similar manner at this point, but it requires a truly uninhibited attitude!)
- When the body is relaxed or "shaken out," **begin to roll up** with your knees relaxed and the top of your head parallel with the floor. Roll up as slowly as you rolled down. The key to a successful roll-down is a slow, thorough approach. As the torso is raised, the arms and shoulders will fall back into place. Last, the head is raised. The end of the exercise should be accompanied by a sense of "lift" in the upper body. Some people say that they feel as though little pockets of space have been created along their spinal column and in their rib cage.

It is now possible to see how the roll-down exercise "warms up" the body's muscles in much the same way that a trained singer "warms up" the voice before performing. The exercise requires little space, time, and privacy. It is adaptable to almost any level of physical ability; at any given time, one need only stretch muscles as far as they are willing to go. While is may be used several times a day to achieve an optimal state of somatic relaxation/focus, it is essential that it be used once a day and that it precede every performance. As stewards of God-given instruments, it is incumbent upon those who stand in the pulpit to be at least as faithful as those who occupy the choir stall.

VARIATIONS ON THE ROLL-DOWN

The adding of voice to the neck roll portion of the roll-down may be used to increase the scope of the exercise. After the neck roll has begun to relax the muscles of the neck, vocalized vowel sounds may be added to warm up the voice (vocal folds and supporting musculature) as well. Running slowly through the long vowels sounds, *a, ee, i, o, u,* enables the exerciser to experiment with breath control, placement, and resonance while preparing the physical apparatus to do its best work.

When a partner is used in the roll-down exercise, several options are added. The most important role for the partner is the guiding of the lowering and raising of the torso, as outlined above. However, the partner may also help the exerciser by providing nonverbal coaching. With a light touch the partner may let the exerciser know that a shoulder is lifting during the neck roll or that an arm needs more stretching. The partner might touch areas of muscles on the back as a way of encouraging the exerciser to target them for tensing/releasing relaxation.

In addition, the partner may offer the exerciser a chance to add a "rag-doll" option to the roll-down. In this part of the exercise, the partner stands behind the exerciser; and after the arm, back, hand, and face muscles are relaxed, the partner circles the exerciser's waist with one arm and gently swings him or her from side to side. Even a small partner can easily swing a large exerciser, provided that the partner takes a wide stance (feet more than shoulders' width apart) and the exerciser has done a thorough job of relaxing.

OTHER EXERCISES

- Leg stretches target the strategically important large muscles of the lower body. Any movement that a preacher might need to perform in the context of preaching is likely to involve this muscle group. Even the small leg movements that typically occur inside the confines of the traditional pulpit can benefit from the warming and "readiness" that stretching creates. This is true because preparing the body to preach involves more than just the kind of muscle-warming that prevents injury in athletes. Preparation for preaching is aimed toward conditioning muscles to be *ready to move*. The goal is muscles that are so responsive that even a small impulse will come to (appropriate, natural and read-able) physical expression.
- Certain simple yoga exercises may be incorporated into the preacher's daily routine with great benefit. The plough, cobra, arch, and candle may be used, for example, to achieve that desirable state of mind and body where relaxation and focus balance and enhance each other. The advantage of adding such exercises to a daily regimen is that they make it possible to extend, prolong, and practice maintaining the psycho-physical state that is the preacher's goal.
- Exercises that provide the opportunity to explore rhythmic movement can also be a valuable part of a preacher's basic training. Rhythmic movement not only gives the muscles a chance to stretch, it gives the preacher's kinesthetic sensibility a chance to take center stage. When the conscious, rational mind steps back and lets the body's sensibilities have freer reign, however temporarily, many preachers find a new range of creativity and expressiveness is the result.

Basic training for performance focuses on the physical preparation of the voice and body. Freedom, flexibility, and responsiveness are the goals. In this approach, the stewardship of God's gifts is emphasized; to be at their best, the vocal apparatus and body must be brought into a state of readiness. A psycho-physical state of readiness is the foundation for a sensitive, natural and appropriate performance of the text. Such a state of readiness is required for the kind of three-dimensional, lively preaching on which we have set our hearts.

Chapter Four

Performing the Text

Whether the text performed is the day's Scripture lesson or the sermon manuscript itself, there are performance rules and rules of thumb that can make the difference between a live word and a dead speech. It might even be said that there are one or two principles that can make as much as a 50 percent difference, just in themselves. It certainly is the case that a number of the rubrics that undergird performance are relatively easy to teach and learn. It will be the aim of this chapter to show how the good and efficient use of such smart rules can help produce enlivened and embodied sermons.

However, as much difference as a few good rules can make, they cannot bring a text to life. Only a faithful interpreter can do that. Faithful interpretation is a function of integrity, exegesis, and self-knowledge. It is fueled by desire and sometimes by love. It involves the giving of self.

••• THE PERFORMER AS INTERPRETER •••

Both the biblical text and the sermon text are arrested performances until that moment in the Sunday morning worship hour when they are performed for and with the assembled congregation. It is the preacher's job to continue the life of the text—to offer it to the hearer with the freshness and immediacy that began at its inception.

This means more than womping up energy and enthusiasm and more than foisting a general intensity onto the text in the vague hope that that will simulate "life." Continuing or resuming the life of an arrested performance means taking responsibility not only for the energy and effectiveness of the physical voice but for interpretation and incarnation.

It is the preacher's job to perform the text for the congregation in such a way that it will slip directly from the listener's ear to the brain. It is not the preacher's job to tell the listener's brain what to think. However, it is the responsibility of the preacher to remove all foreseeable impediments to the listener's ear. The preacher's goal is to deliver the text to the listener's ear shaped in such a way that it will be possible for the listener to take it in quickly and begin his or her own (mental, emotional, spiritual) work of digestion.

It is the preacher's job to make some decisions about which pieces of the text deserve priority, about which aspects of the text should be divided from each other and which are important to keep linked. The preacher decides what layers of connotative meaning can be added and what rhythm and meter are most consonant with the text's life. Likewise, it is the job of the preacher to sniff out the shape of the text, to see where it peaks and what devices it uses to build momentum to reach that point. Obviously it is also the preacher who decides which part of her or his face and body will carry forward the life of the text. The preacher runs the text through his or her own internal circuits as it comes out his or her mouth. The preacher does all of these things whether she or he means to or not. The only question is whether the preacher will be purposeful or thoughtless about the doing.

There are, of course, people who read the Scripture and preach who consciously adhere to what they call a "neutral" reading style. Often out of a deep respect for the text (this approach usually focuses on the reading of Scripture, although a few proponents may apply the principle to preaching as well), these readers/preachers aim to deliver a "pure" reading of the text. They see the job description of the reader/preacher as that of a reading machine. The reader's goal, in this view, is to get the words off the page and out into the air without adding a jot or tittle to them. These readers aim for as plain a reading of the text as is possible, in the belief that each listener should be allowed to make his or her own interpretation.

The problem with this approach, of course, is that there is no such thing as a reading that is not an interpretation. The text as it exists on the page has already been subject to at least one layer of interpretation. It has been translated—and it may have been emended, redacted, and edited, as well. The act of oral performance inevitably adds another layer of interpretation. Once a reader starts picking the words up off the page and sending them out into the air with his or her voice, she or he is interpreting. (Even what seems to be a given about the text often involves a subtle decision on the part of the reader. The reader chooses, for example, whether to pause at commas or only for the purposes of breathing. Such a decision can, in some cases, be an important interpretive decision.) There is no noninterpretation option; there is only the choice between being in charge of the interpretation or hapless about it.

✦✦✦ VOCALICS: THE ART OF ORCHESTRATION ✦✦✦

The foundation of a careful, skilled performance may be said to be comprised of four basic materials: rate, pitch, volume, and (the use of) pause. These elements of oral performance are known as "vocalics." Ideally, the control of these elements creates a reading that is orchestrated to match (and, therefore, express or animate) the moves and rhythms of the text.

The name of the vocalics game is variety. The skillful interpreter combines and recombines these four elements of oral communication to express the life of the text, never staying with any one combination long enough for it to bore the listener's ear. Of course, the reader/preacher's decisions about the changing combinations are cued not by some anxious desire to keep the listener's attention, but by the text. The ultimate purpose of the four building blocks is to interpret and express the life of the text. In general and for example:

- a fast rate, rising pitch, high volume, no-pause combination can express a text's acceleration or increasing intensity: "My heart says to Thee, hide not Thy face from me; Cast me not away."
- a slow rate, low pitch, low volume, long/frequent pause combination can express the meditative quality of another text: "He maketh me to lie down in green pastures, He leadeth me beside still waters, He restoreth my soul...."
- a moderate rate, low pitch, low volume, no-pause combination can help convey a text's menacing feel: "Mene, mene, tekel, upharsin."
- a slow rate, low pitch, high volume, short pause combination can communicate something of the text's agony: "My God, My God, why hast Thou forsaken me?"

The possibilities for combining and recombining rate, pitch, volume, and pause to create different effects are nearly endless. While they should not be applied to the text in a mechanical or haphazard way, experimenting with these four speech-regulators can help a faithful interpreter find and orchestrate the music of the text.

Such a process begins with rehearsal. The only way to make responsible decisions about orchestration is by exploring the options with voice and body—starting early and continuing to return to the experiment—throughout the sermon preparation process. There is no such thing as a silent rehearsal. There is no such thing as a sedentary rehearsal. In order to begin the kind of creative work that this chapter describes, the preacher's voice and body must be activated.

✦✦✦ PHRASING: THE ART OF PAUSE ✦✦✦

A phrase in oral communication—as in music—is a unit of meaning. For the purpose of oral reading, a phrase may be defined as a group of words that expresses a thought, image, or movement. Every sentence is comprised of at least one phrase. Some phrases are enhanced when a reader pauses after them, some are not. The trick is in knowing one kind of sentence from another.

The twin aims of careful phrasing are (1) to keep related

thoughts grouped together and (2) to allow the listener such short periods of silence, pauses, as are necessary in order for the listener to absorb the message. A general awareness of these goals will go a long way in guiding the sensitive reader/preacher in the use of pause. However, there are a few famous pitfalls worth warning beginners about—and reminding old hands of.

1. Never phrase at the opening of quotation marks. If you could only remember one rule of phrasing, this would be the one to choose. Whenever you are reading Scripture in church on Sunday morning and come to a comma that is followed by quotation marks, a red flag should go up in you mind: *do not pause.* It may go against every instinct and every model you have ever had, but don't do it. A pause throws back the listener's attention to the word immediately preceding it. Do you really think that the word *said* or *saying* is worth highlighting? See how much more easily the sense of the sentence is conveyed if you step on that connecting word as you would on a bar of soap. Step on it and slide into the meat of the quote. Keep the listener focused on the substance, not the stage directions.

Common: Jesus opened his mouth and taught them saying, (pause) "Blessed are the merciful."

Better: Jesus opened his mouth (pause) and taught them saying, "Blessed are the merciful." Or: Jesus opened his mouth and taught them (pause) saying, "Blessed are the merciful."

2. Don't be a respecter of commas. In general, do not let punctuation make your phrasing decisions for you. The speech teachers' old saw that "punctuation directs the eye to meaning and phrasing directs the ear" is especially useful in the reading of Scripture. Punctuation helps the reader make sense of the text, but may or may not give him or her good advice about how to package the message for the ear. Not every period deserves a fat pause. Some are better ignored. Some of the best-placed pauses occur where there is no comma, semicolon, colon, quotation mark, question mark, exclamation point, or period in sight. The reader must make phrasing decisions based on what the text wants to say, not the way it is decorated on the page.

3. Never phrase before a vocative.   Among the most painful phrasing mistakes in oral Scripture reading is the mishandling of a vocative. Examples abound.

Common: "Great is thy faithfulness (pause) O God my maker."
Better: "Great is thy faithfulness O God my maker." (Said without a pause, this makes it clear that the praise for someone's faithfulness is addressed to God.)
Effective: "Great (pause) is thy faithfulness O God my maker."
In this case, the pause causes the first word to be emphasized.)
Common: "Lift up your heads (pause) O ye gates."
Better: "Lift up your heads O ye gates" (said without a pause).
Common: "Deliver me (pause) O Lord from evildoers."
Better: "Deliver me O Lord, (pause) from evildoers."
Common: "I beseech you therefore (pause) brothers and sisters (pause) that you present your bodies a living sacrifice."
Better: "I beseech you therefore brothers and sisters (pause) that you present your bodies...."

The rule to remember is that the vocative ("O, Somebody" or a direct address like the "brothers and sisters" above) clings to what comes before it.

4. Other famous phrasing mistakes:

• The line "And they came with haste, and found Mary and Joseph and the Babe lying in the manger." is often read in such a way as to make it sound as if all three members of the Holy Family were wedged into the feeding trough together. If the reader pauses after "Joseph" but does not pause after "Babe," this problem can be avoided.
• The last line of the Lord's Prayer, when prayed corporately, is

often phrased with a pause after "power," giving the impression that of all God's attributes only "glory" is "forever." If the line is read or the line of the prayer is prayed without pausing, the theology is better.

- The meaning of Ruth's famous line can be nearly inverted with a misplaced pause. "Entreat me (pause) not to leave thee" makes it sound as if Ruth is asking Naomi to beg her to stay. To convey the intended meaning—that is, of Ruth saying to Naomi, "Don't ask me to leave you"—the pause must be placed after "not."

The purpose of paying attention to phrasing is to create the sound of natural speaking patterns. While it would be ideal for readers to be able to rely on their instincts to reproduce the sound of spontaneous speech, these skills do not come to most of us automatically. Think of how difficult it can be to "just be yourself" when somebody holding a video camera tells you to. It can be hard to remember how to "be natural." Something similar happens to many people when they pick up a text to read it out loud. Most people need to practice applying the kind of guidelines offered above to their oral reading.

On the other hand, it is important that the rules offered be taken as heuristic devices. The goal is natural, honest, enlivened speech. Applying rules in a legalistic or over-zealous manner can lead to the very kind of mechanical performance most readers are trying to avoid. What is important is not the preciseness with which the reader applies these principles, but the degree to which they help the reader discover and convey the meaning of the text.

✦✦ EMPHASIS: THE ART OF PRIORITIZING ✦✦

Of all the techniques that can turn a dead reading into an enlivened performance, perhaps the single most important is the skillful use of emphasis. The great American elocutionist Leland Powers described the goal. "A word is emphasized when it is lifted into prominence in order to arrest attention. . . . Emphasis is used to discriminate the important from all related ideas."[1]

Stanislavski preferred the term "accentuation" for the same

technique and had a somewhat more colorful way of describing its effect. "The accent is a pointing finger. It singles out the key word in a phrase or measure. In the word thus underscored we shall find the soul, the inner essence, the high point of the subtext."[2]

Other schools of acting refer to this discipline as finding the text's "operative words." There are many possible approaches; but for the purposes of this discussion, it will be helpful to think in terms of prioritizing. The goal for the reader/preacher is the creation of appropriate emphasis patterns that approximate natural speech. Every performer can develop his or her "ear" for emphasis.

An example will serve to launch the discussion. Read the line "I never said she stole my purse" putting the emphasis on the first word. Control the reading of all the other words in the sentence so only the word *I* is stressed. Now read the same line a second time, reserving the emphasis for only the second word. Make sure only the word *never* is lifted into prominence. Continue the exercise by repeating the line, each time emphasizing a different word, subduing the inflection of all other words except the single word that is emphasized. You see how the meaning conveyed is different in each instance.

"*I* never said she stole my purse."
(Maybe someone else said it.)

"I *never* said she stole my purse."
(I didn't say it before, I'm not saying it now.)

"I never *said* she stole my purse."
(I may have implied it.)

"I never said *she* stole my purse."
(It was someone else altogether.)

"I never said she *stole* my purse."
(Now that I think about it, she might have just borrowed it.)

"I never said she stole *my* purse."
(But someone else might have been victimized.)

"I never said she stole my *purse*."
(It was my wallet I was complaining about.)

The rule-of-thumb for deciding which word deserves the priority, in any given instance, is this: *the word that carries the meaning of the sentence forward is emphasized.* There are two common ways that meaning is carried forward: by the introduction of something new and by the introduction of something being contrasted. For example, the Old Testament text,

"Then Elijah said to all the people, 'Come near to me.'
And all the people came near to him." (I Kings 18:30)

is often read with the emphasis on *near* in the first line and *near* in the second line. But notice how much more easily the picture of Elijah and the Israelites enters the ear and comes up on the listener's mental motion-picture screen when *came* is emphasized in the second line.

"Then Elijah said to all the people, 'Come *near* to me.'
And all the people *came* near to him."

How do we know it will work better this way? Because, according to the rule of thumb being advanced here, new ideas are emphasized and old ideas are subdued. *Near,* by the time it occurs in the second line, is an old idea; the fact that the people of Israel actually did what he asked them to do (a fact that is communicated by the word *came*) is the new idea.

Similarly, when Jesus says,

"Peace I leave with you.
My peace give I unto you.
Not as the world gives, give I unto you." (John 14:27)

See how much more quickly the listener absorbs the meaning when *peace* is emphasized in the first line, *my* in the second and *world/I* in the third. In this example, both guidelines are operative: the emphasized words are introducing not only something that is new but something that is being contrasted.

"*Peace* I leave with you
My peace I give unto you
Not as the *world* gives, give *I* unto you."

In the reading of Scripture and preaching, there are certain words that seldom deserve emphasis. General words that indicate place or time—*here, there, that place, now, then*—often get a priority that they don't deserve. Unless they are being contrasted (i.e., with another place or another time) or are the point of the sentence, they do not carry the meaning forward. Certain common adverbs and adjectives—*very, really, big, all*—tempt us to fall into the kind of over-inflected speech patterns we relied upon to keep our three-year-old's interest through a long fairy tale.

Similarly, prepositions, though they are quite widely emphasized in common practice, seldom further the meaning of a sentence. Look again at Jesus' benediction in John 14:27. The first line gets the most important notion of all on the table: *peace*. It will be enough just to stress that word. Though it may be tempting to also emphasize either *leave* or *you,* a review of the immediate literary context will show that neither one is nearly as important as the priority on communicating *peace*: "*Peace* I leave with you."

As has been said, prioritizing in the second line is determined by the guideline which directs that contrasted words be emphasized. Although *my* is the most important word to stress in line two, many readers are tempted to emphasize *unto* as well. However, the line is better interpreted: "*My* peace I give unto you."

Some readers even succumb to the preposition when it occurs again in the third line. Again, the preposition *unto* should be subdued and the line read: "Not as the *world* gives, give *I* unto you."

The temptation to emphasize prepositions like the ones above, which do nothing to carry the meaning of the sentence forward, may be based on a desire to appear neutral or unemotional—or to distance oneself from the import of the text. It may also be the result of a habit absorbed from listening to other speakers in public and private settings. Giving prepositions more than their due has become quite commonplace. On a recent flight, the attendant's voice came over the intercom during the descent, announcing that we would "be landing *in* Phoenix." ("As opposed to *under* Phoenix?" I thought.) Any day of the week, one might hear a television commentator with a bright, lively style signing off his segment of the evening program with something like, "See you tomorrow with more *from* the news desk." In a tense boardroom debate, a junior partner might be heard saying, "This is an important plan, *in* the long run."

Whatever the reason that Scripture readers and preachers emphasize prepositions and other undeserving words, it is clear that such decisions are not made consciously. A conscious refocusing of attention to what furthers the sense of the sentence will help the reader/preacher make more effective choices. Better yet, a seasoned performer will develop his or her ability to "internalize" the text—to think the author's thoughts along with the words, as the words come out of the reader's mouth. This ability to "be present in the words," or to be absorbed in the "what" of what one is reading, is largely a function of desire and concentration. More will be said about this key discipline later.

••• PAINTING THE PICTURE: THE NONVERBAL ARTS •••

Where to place emphasis? Great point!

It is one thing to decide where to put the emphasis in a given sentence and another to know how to create that emphasis. Stress, pitch, vowel extension, and pause all may be used to lift a word into prominence. In Western cultures, each of these ways of creating emphasis is associated with a particular mode or style of speech. A theory describing the correspondence between three literary genres and the nonverbal techniques that are most effective in bringing each type of literature to life was formulated nearly a century ago by the ingenious elocutionist Leland Powers. He referred to the schemata he developed as "The Trinity of Expression."[3]

Powers theorized that any piece of literature could be categorized as one of three genres, based on the text's rhetorical appeal. In the Bible, for example, a given passage may be seen to appeal to either the rational, emotional, or kinesthetic faculties of readers. Powers acknowledged that two or even all three appeals might be found in a single pericopae, but argued that one would always be dominant. Knowing which appeal is dominant is crucial for the oral interpreter, Powers believed, since each genre of literature is most effectively interpreted by different speech techniques.

What Powers believed to be true about texts—that each may be noted to have a dominant mode or style of communication—may be seen to apply as well to the people who read the texts. Most readers have a dominant mode that may be said to be the home base from which they read the Scripture. The readers who are most comfortable with snappy arguments tend also to have a natural ability to use the delivery techniques that are most effective in conveying snappy arguments. The vocal and nonverbal devices they use most easily tend to be the very ones that are consonant with argumentation. This would be true as well of the readers who are more comfortable with images that call up emotions and with the ones who seem to prefer the swashbuckling stories that set the muscles twitching. Readers tend to have a home base and to use the techniques of that home base instinctively, naturally. The problem occurs when a reader transports the techniques that work so well in his or her home base to one of the other two modes.

For those whose job it is to prepare and perform the public reading of Scripture (and their own sermon manuscripts), Powers' theory and the corollary suggested above can provide valuable guidelines. Of course, Powers' schemata should never be used as a substitute for the kind of rehearsal disciplines that have already been presented; however, when his approach is used as a heuristic tool to open up the reader's experience of the text, it can be quite effective. Not only can these guidelines help prime the performer's pump, they can provide a valuable safeguard or check against the unconscious mixing of nonverbal messages.

1. HEAD-ORIENTED PEOPLE

People who are dominantly reflective by nature—who may feel more comfortable with the Apostle Paul's contributions to the canon, for example—are also likely to be people who create emphasis with pitch. Preferring, as they tend to do, literature that moves from thought to thought or idea to idea, they themselves move from thought to thought by way of linear thinking. For them the use of pitch (or inflection patterns) is an elegant and supremely effective way to highlight what is important in the text without hindering the flow of ideas.

In addition, the nonverbal behavior of this group tends to have several predictable characteristics: eye-movement is used to show thinking, gestures that feature fingertips are preferred and vocalics tend toward the short, quick, and clipped. Head-oriented readers often catch on quickly to the art of emphasis, feeling at home as they do with the world of analysis and abstract reasoning.

2. HEART-ORIENTED PEOPLE

People who are dominantly emotion-oriented, whose taste in Scripture runs, perhaps, to the Psalms and laments, are likely to create emphasis through vowel extension or use of pause. "What a sweeeet baaaby," they say when they meet you and Junior on the sidewalk, and similarly, "I will dweeell in the houuuse of the Looord forever." Alternatively, the heart-oriented reader may use more and fatter pauses, usually locating them after the word they wish to emphasize and providing the listener the "space" they need to absorb the emotional impact of what is being read.

Pericopaes that may be categorized as dominantly heart-oriented (the Psalms, for example) move not from idea to idea, but from image to image. It is word-pictures, not ideas, that express and evoke emotion. A heart-oriented text moves from one image and the emotion it elicits to the next. The nonverbal behaviors that are associated with heart-oriented people and texts focus on the reader's cheeks and palms. The heart-oriented make themselves more vulnerable than others. Politicians, for example, often favor a more "protected" gesture—like the soft fist gesture used by JFK and Bill Clinton, or the slicing palm (finger tips forward, palm facing to the side) used by Mario Cuomo. The displaying of an open palm—extended toward the audience as a gospel singer might, or raised in benediction—signals an emotional openness. Similarly, it is easy to see that a speaker who keeps the cheeks of his or her face impassive is not likely to be a heart-oriented reader. This group is full of readers who find it necessary to wrinkle, lift, moue, and dimple their countenances in order to convey every nuance of emotion they feel.

3. GUT-ORIENTED PEOPLE

People who are dominantly action-oriented—often the same people who prefer the sweeping Cecil B. De Mille type stories of the Old Testament—are likely to create emphasis by putting stress or force on the prioritized word. Since stories unfold scene by scene, not primarily by the movement of thought or poetic imagery, they rely on a kind of rhythm to achieve their goal. It makes a certain kind of sense that the reader would use a "downbeat" stress or force to work in concert with the text's rhythms.

It is said that the action-oriented reader connects with the story on a gut level because such readers are able to establish a kinesthetic tie to the text. They see it unfold in their mind's eye and experience it in "muscle memory" as they narrate the tale. In particular, it is the trunk of the reader's body and the back of the arm that are set tingling by these Big Stories. Movement of the upper body and large, sweeping gestures featuring full arm extension are characteristic of this group's nonverbal communication. The athlete's classic gesture of triumph, which consists of a bent-arm suddenly jerked downward and backward, is a hallmark of this group's style.

✦✦✦ INTERNALIZATION ✦✦✦

More than a half century ago, the preacher's theologian H. H. Farmer summed up the difference between preaching and "mere reading":

> Merely to read the sermon is fatal. It is worse than fatal; it is the culpable repudiation of one's task and calling. . . . The alternative to reading is not dispensing entirely with notes or manuscript in the pulpit. The alternative to reading is *preaching* and you *can* preach from notes and even from a full manuscript if you have taken the trouble to . . . absorb it.[4]

The same may be said about the difference between the performed word (whether of Scripture or sermon) and the word that is merely read. The ability to be absorbed in the "what" of what one is reading or preaching is a function of one's ability to internalize the text. When a head-oriented text is internalized, it is run through the reader's cerebral circuits as—or a split second before—it comes out of the reader's mouth. A Psalm is circulated through the reader's own emotional center as it comes out of his or her mouth. Similarly, when a gut-oriented reader interprets an epic story, the story is recreated on the reader's mental screen and the reader's muscles resonate with the words as they leave his or her lips.

The alternatives to internalization are several and deadly. Many readers/preachers pick the print up off the page with their eyes and run it out their mouths and are satisfied that they have done their job. They are reading machines, not preachers. The words never come anywhere near the center of life, and it shows. The text emerges from the mouths of such readers sterile, misshapen, dead.

Other preachers settle for slathering the reading of the Scripture or sermon with a layer of emotional mayonnaise. One deep dip in the jar, one pass of the knife, and the result is an obscured text and a monotonous texture. The common holy-drone and predictable inflection pattern that is characteristic of much mainline preaching is enough to make anyone gag. Hollywood stereotypes it, Generation Xers mock it, Boomers avoid it. And they are right. This kind of "attitudinizing" has done as much as anything to give preaching a bad name and to cause the faithful to worry about sermons that are "merely performances." The irony is that the very preachers who cause the words "performance" and "acting" to be stigmatized are themselves, at most, *bad* actors, *bad* performers. Some would say they do not deserve to be called actors or performers at all.

There are still others who read Scripture and preach whose *modus operandi* is to search out what they judge to be key words in the text and pantomime them. "Our Father," they read pretending to bow their heads, "Who art in heaven" (up-pointed finger accompanies the raising of the head). "Hallowed be" (hands folded) "thy name" (head bowed again). "Thy kingdom come" (head raised expectantly), "thy will be done on earth" (arm sweeps out horizontally) "as it is in" (up-pointed finger) "heaven." Of all the substitutions for internalization this one may frustrate the listener most. It represents a singular lack of imagination on the part of the interpreter and reduces the embodiment of the text to an embarrassing kind of verbal diagram. It reminds one of the kind of silly sign-language desperate tourists fall into when they are unable to speak the language of the country in which they are traveling. It is difficult to imagine what such interpreters hope to add to the text. Do they think that the listener's experience of the text will be enhanced by hand-signals pointing out the direction of the heavens? Do they imagine that the listener's receiving of the text will be enlarged by gestures that are every bit as verbal as the words they are meant to . . . illustrate?! To add insult to injury the listener/viewer of this melange of verbal messages is often subjected not only to corny, mechanical, literalistic movement but to *movement that comes a beat late*—movement that *follows* instead of accompanies the thought impulse that gives rise to it. How much better (simpler, cleaner, more natural) it is to actually think the thought and feel the impulse and to let the arms and hands express those impulses. Not only will it feel more natural to the interpreter, but it will look more natural to its audience and will avoid reducing the text to the level of a Sunday school ditty with hand motions.

✦✦✦ COMMON PROBLEMS WITH THE PERFORMED WORD ✦✦✦

For those whose job it is to bring arrested texts to life on Sunday morning, there are several pitfalls that bear mentioning. All of these are quite common. All are distracting; some are deadly. All deserve to be red flagged.

1. *Slow and steady does not win the race.* Often when listeners react to a reader or speaker with distaste, they mislabel the speaker as a "monotone." In fact, there are far fewer true monotones than there are mono-rates. Reading at a too-steady rate is a nearly ubiquitous problem. It may well be that a slow and steady rate is the most common oral interpretative problem of all.

Natural speech is downright erratic compared to the way many people read. Full of explosive starts, sudden stops, side trips, spurts, jogs, and even foot dragging, natural speech moves forward unevenly. Its rhythms are endlessly interesting, and they do the crucial job of packaging content into hearable bits. Pauses of varying length, sometimes in surprising places, keep listeners' attention and give them time to digest what is being communicated. In addition, the average listener can listen much more quickly than most speakers can speak. As long as a speaker's diction is crisp enough to support a fast rate, she or he should have no concern about its judicious use.

2. Don't make the crooked straight. Many preachers seem to approach oral reading with a kind of a John the Baptist mentality. It is as if they are searching out all the precious peaks, hills, ridges, mounds, dunes, and mesas of the text in order to mow them down. Gullies and canyons are filled in. Turns and twists are smoothed out. The problem is that in the process of making all the text's rough places into plains, these prophets manage to bulldoze the life right out of the text.

Peaks and valleys are indispensable to the ear. Varied levels of intensity are so important in expressing the sense and animus of a text that they should be sought out, cherished, and rejoiced over. If they didn't exist, the reader would have to invent them. It's unthinkable that a skilled reader would throw away the text's own perfectly good levels. Effective oral interpreters lean into a text's intensity levels, going with the flow of life when it wants to build, and sliding back when it wants to rest.

3. Avoid the stained-glass-window voice. There is a very funny joke about a pastor who intones a long and overly personal story in the same voice that he uses for preaching. Of course the joke cannot be told here. Intonation patterns do not translate easily into print. If they did, some speech teacher would have published something by now that would effectively wipe out the classic intonation pattern that plagues American and British pulpits.

No one who has been to church more than twice in his or her life can be in the dark about what intoning sounds like. Imagine six syllables spoken quickly at a slightly higher than average pitch and a seventh dropped to a slightly lower than average pitch and sustained for three beats. This is one of the more common intonation patterns. When this kind of a pattern is imposed onto a religious text, a modern classic results: the stained-glass-window voice.

The preacher is striving, often unconsciously, for a holy sound and for a voice that is different from her or his everyday voice. But intoning is a cheap out for an interpreter. And what is cheap in terms of the investment of the interpreter is expensive in terms of the text's effectiveness. This kind of arbitrary imposition of pitch and rhythm patterns works not *with* the sense of the text to enliven it, but *against* the sense of the text, killing it.

✦✦✦ THE UNSELFISH PERFORMER ✦✦✦

The difference between a faithful performer and a schlocky performer has something to do with the performer's willingness to practice certain disciplines. A commitment to rehearsal, the careful application of such oral interpretation guidelines as are outlined above and the honest desire to connect with a text through the process of internalization go a long way toward predicting the effectiveness of an oral performance—whether it is Scripture or sermon text that is being interpreted. However, there is another difference between faithful preachers and schlocky preachers that is as important as the techniques they practice. Faithful preachers, as faithful actors, handle the texts they interpret with respect, even reverence.

Where preaching is an art and not merely entertainment or propaganda, the difference may often be traced to a difference of attitude toward (or commitment to) the biblical text. The artist-preacher is one who is willing to enter into a profound partnership with the text. The faithful preacher strives for a process of dialogue, discovery, and synthesis with the text; mastery, dominance, and penetration of the text are eschewed. The resulting sermons are as full of the voice and life of the text as they are full of the voice and personality of the preacher. Sermons preached by selfish preachers will always look and sound different from sermons preached by preachers who deal faithfully with the text. It is true in theatre, as well.

In the classic *How's Your Second Act?* Arthur Hopkins observes that an actor or playwright cannot hide an egotistical approach to his or her work—the truth will out. As Hopkins shows, the attitude that is necessary to both good theatre and good preaching is an attitude of self-giving.

> Author, director, scene designer, and actor must become completely the servants of the play.... Each must make himself a free, transparent medium through which the whole flows freely.... It requires a complete surrender of selfishness.[5]

> This kind of self-giving, as actors know, is first of all a function of love. In the first place, I would have him [critic, author, actor, artist, director] love the theatre, and in the second place, I would have him liberated from any desire to be personally effective in connection with it.[6]

Also associated with this approach is a kind of self-forgetting. The actor/performer/preacher is so absorbed in the "what" of what she or he is saying, that the "what" takes up all available space within the performer. The "how," "why," and "who" recede. This may be what the great Constantin Stanislavski himself envisioned when he gave his famous advice, "Love the art in your self, not yourself in the art."[7]

✦✦✦ A HERMENEUTIC FOR THE PERFORMED WORD ✦✦✦

If we say that African American preaching is often shaped by a "hermeneutic of the cross" and that it is common for feminist preachers to use a "hermeneutic of the resurrection," we might also say that the interpretive principle that underlies this incarnational approach to preaching employs a "hermeneutic of annunciation." Such a hermeneutic would require of the performer the kind of unselfish attitude outlined above and certain additional commitments:

1. a respect for the text.
2. an openness to the voice of the text.
3. a willingness to subordinate his or her will—not to the text— but to the will of the text to become itself.[8]

The historical model for such an approach is obvious.

The Word became flesh through a human act of receptivity, availability, and profound cooperation. When the human person Mary of Nazareth responded to the possibility of Incarnation, she said, in the old language, "Be it done unto me according to thy word." By her own affirmative words she allowed the Word to take upon itself the flesh of her flesh. The holy interpreter is like Mary in allowing the word to be born.[9]

In the case of the reader and preacher of Scripture, the incarnational process begins with "respecting" the text. Prayer, translation work, and textual criticism might accompany the reader's experimentation with embodying the text, for example. Some preachers might also "reverence the text" with incense or elevation or the sign of the cross. For others, standing or kneeling during their initial reading of the text makes sense, body posture reminding the reader of the holiness of the task. Others find that large-muscle repetitive movement such as pacing keeps them focused on the voice of the text.

Lectio divina, currently enjoying a resurgence of popular interest, has a long track record of helping Christian preachers open themselves to the voice of the text. When practiced in concert with exegetical efforts and the application of various critical tools, it can lead a preacher to new discoveries—even in texts that have become quite familiar. Minimally, opening oneself to the voice of the text, involves an inquiring spirit and a willingness to, at least momentarily, set aside one's own agenda. While it is not possible for a reader to still his or her own internal voice(s) entirely, the motivated preacher will find ways to let the text's voice emerge out of the melee.

Subordinating oneself to the text is a technique that is not recommended in this approach. Self-giving has its place in the process of annunciation, but its role is limited. Self-giving follows a period of listening and pondering, and it stops when it means loss of self. Self-sacrifice stops when it means sacrificing identity. The limit of subordination is reached when the reader's integrity is threatened. After all, the goal of this annunciation is incarnation: the combination of two separate entities that produces a third, which embodies them both and *in which the integrity of each is still preserved.*

Annunciation requires respect, openness, and subordination, but what the interpreter subordinates himself or herself to is not the text but the will of the text to become itself. In addition, the subordinating is temporary and chosen. This kind of inviting the text to take the stage enables the interpreter to enter into a partnership with the life of the text. If the reader is seen as one who releases the life of the text, then "subordination" may be seen as a simple, graceful act of stepping back—of making room—of getting oneself out of Gabriel's way.

Chapter Five

What Actors Know

In the legitimate theatre there are good actors and bad actors, great artists and schlocky performers. There are actors who hold a cynical view of their craft and those who see in their art a high calling. Just as is the case for preachers, some actors are more talented, creative, and well trained than others. What actors know varies from person to person and school to school. But all effective actors know some things. In this chapter I claim that some of what actors know could do preachers a world of good.

The following discussion focuses on the disciplines and values of theatrical artists that preachers may find useful in the practice of their own art. It is not my purpose here to reprise what has already been said about the mechanics of the craft, i.e., about vocal projection and the judicious use of emphasis in oral interpretation. In this chapter I will attempt to show that there are many things in the actor's bag of tricks that the preacher might like to have in hers or his. Some of the items in that bag have to do with the particular disciplines that undergird the creative process, and some have to do with a certain ethos, a set of norms and values that are widely held in the theatre and that suggest a course for preachers and worshipers.

This chapter will recap some of the body of knowledge that is shared by artistic actors, that is, by those who hold a high view of their art and who practice the kind of disciplined self-giving described in the previous chapter. This kind of devotion to theatre is epitomized in such schools as the "Poor Theatre" of Jerzy Growtowski and the "Rough Theatre" of Peter Brook. However, it is not necessary to subscribe to such radical views to be an actor who is dedicated to his or her art. A hybrid middle-of-the-road approach, which takes as its baseline the "Method" Constantin Stanislavski brought to America in 1922 (by the "Russian Revolution" in the form of the Moscow Art Theater) and which includes gleanings from its critics as well as its heirs, will serve as well for our purposes.

••• BASIC ELEMENTS OF THE CREATIVE PROCESS •••

Three intertwined disciplines form the foundation of the artist's creative process. Writers, painters, and sculptors are as well acquainted with them as actors and directors. Preaching requires their use as well, but it may be that preachers are less likely to have named the steps that take them through the familiar routine. When we preachers do think about our creative process—on a Thursday morning perhaps, when sermon composition is not moving smoothly—what is it we would say we need in order to be more creative? Is it perhaps "intuition" or "talent" or "spontaneous insight" we wish to have more of? In fact, all of those things may be developed. All of them are aspects of creativity, and all of them are innate in preachers.

Creativity may be defined simply as the bringing of something new into the world. "It is catching and holding fast a fleeting moment of truth in a painting, a piece of clay, or a poem. It is discovering a new interpretation or taking something that already exists and changing it in an unpredictable way."[1] Certainly the work that preachers do is creative work. Although they do not create *ex nihilo,* there is nonetheless "something new" involved. Preachers are concerned, as are actors, with the truthful interpretation of texts. This interpretative process is, as has been said, a generative and incarnational activity. Something new is born out of the coming together of text and interpreter, something in which the integrity of each is still preserved.

Ultimately creativity is the product of experience. We might say creative talent derives from experiencing experience. As the great acting teacher Viola Spolin says:

> We must reconsider what is meant by *talent*. It is highly possible that what is called talented behavior is simply a greater individual capacity for experiencing. From this point of view, it is in the increasing of the individual capacity for experiencing that the untold potentiality of a personality can be evoked.[2]

Spolin claims that the ability to develop creativity is in the reach of every human being—of every sentient creature—of every preacher who is capable of awareness of her or his own experience and who is willing to broaden and deepen it. But being willing to experience your experience is only the starting point in developing creative ability. An openness to what writing teacher Julia Cameron calls "spiritual electricity" is also important. She recounts an aspect of the creative task that is of particular interest to preachers.

> The heart of creativity is an experience of the mystical union; the heart of the mystical union is an experience of creativity. Those who speak in spiritual terms routinely refer to God as the creator but seldom see *creator* as the literal term for artist. I am suggesting you take the term *creator* quite literally. You are seeking to forge a creative alliance, artist-to-artist with the Great Creator. Accepting this concept can greatly expand your creative possibilities.[3]

Of course preachers need not rely on the experience and advice of artists alone; an increasing number of theologians are willing to make a case for creativity. Some even see it as a spiritual enterprise which is fundamental to and universal in human experience. From Jürgen Moltmann to Mary Daly, there is no shortage of theologians and writers on spirituality who see in the *imago dei*, the suggestion that the human capacity for creativity is God-given and reflects God's imprint on our natures.[4] In theological terms, creativity may be understood as a spiritual experience that has its ultimate source in the "God-spark" in us.

Others have observed that this unique element of human nature is characterized by an ability to gain access to the unconscious and by a sense of discovery that is opened by instinct for play. Of these aspects of human creativity, it may be that the role of play is most misunderstood. Johan Huizinga has shown that the human instinct for play is a fundamental element of culture. He defines the term broadly, describing it as

> a voluntary activity or occupation executed within certain fixed limits of time and place, according to rules freely accepted but absolutely binding, having its aim in itself and accompanied by a feeling of tensions, joy and the consciousness that it is "different" from "ordinary life."[5]

Whether one is composing sermons or delivering Shakespeare, an instinct for play fuels the effort. The title of Huizinga's classic text on the subject is suggestive of his findings: *Homo Ludens*. If he is right, the instinct for play is not only universal but is an essential element of human nature. Again, this suggests that the building blocks of creativity are within the grasp of all human beings, or at least within the grasp of all human beings who are willing to play.

Renewed research into the subject of human creativity during the past decade shows that though basic creative ability may be universal, individuals who are especially creative share certain traits. The work of University of Chicago researcher Mihaly Csikzentmihalyi, for example, shows that creative people performing at their peak seem to have an ability to enter another world where time is distorted and a sense of well-being encompasses them. Csikzentmihalyi calls this a state of "flow"—a state of being "alive and fully attentive to what you're doing."[6] One way of understanding such a state is that access to the unconscious is freer and fuller during such times than it is in the ordinary moments of waking life. Another way of understanding it is in spiritual terms as an experience of communion or inspiration. Other traits common among the particularly creative individuals who enjoy such a state include curiosity, openness to new experience, willingness to take risks and a tendency to think in images.[7]

For actors and preachers, all of these qualities may be seen to focus toward one end. "For the interpreter creation is a process of concentrating the inner faculties on an external image . . . and adjusting one's whole being to it."[8] The kind of work that brings actor and text together this way results in what Stanislavski called "creative acting." When such a creative process is fully engaged, a kind of synthesis occurs between actor and text, Stanislavski believed, in which something new is created.

✦✦✦ CONCENTRATION *✦✦✦*

Nothing much of value happens in the study or the pulpit, in creating or performing, apart from the discipline of concentration. The ability to deepen concentration is closely connected to the ability to reap the rich resources of the unconscious mind. Gaining access to the preacher's unconscious is the key step in reaching the hearer's. "Theatre is wholly concerned with the unconscious mind of the audience,"[9] drama critic Arthur Hopkins claims. We might say the same of preaching. Where is the potential for transformation located in the person who listens to a sermon? Where are held the values out of which a human being lives? Where do the images reside that shape who we are and what we do? In the unconscious. In preaching, as in theatre, "deep calls to deep." To reach the depths of the hearer, it is essential that the preacher be able to gain access to her or his own. This access is undergirded by the discipline of concentration.

Actors who follow Stanislavski's method regard concentration as the first and essential discipline. For them concentration consists of paying strong and unwavering attention to the task or the object at hand. The discipline of concentration is comprised of a number of skills, including the ability to still the conscious mind, to eliminate distraction, to focus, to be absorbed in a task, and to create sensory or emotional memory. All of these skills may be cultivated by exercise.

Stanislavski favored observation exercises for the building of concentration. Actually, the term *observation* is used in the Method in a specialized way to designate the particular kind of looking that detects and analyzes human motivation. Used in this more narrow way, the word refers to a disciplined state in which

103

the actor continually keeps before herself or himself the challenge of identifying a person's character and emotion based only on appearance.

However, many of Stanislavski's concentration exercises call for observation in its broader sense; that is, his concentration exercises employ the act of seeing and noting. So, although *observation* and *concentration* have distinct uses in the Method school, we will consider them together here, employing the word *observation* in its broader sense. Much of what the preacher may want to learn about concentration has to do with this kind of observation, that is with the act of paying attention.

There are many stories of how the great master of theatre put young actors through their paces, teaching them to combine relaxation and attentiveness. "That is not looking. It is staring," Stanislavski would chide. "Still a lot of mechanical gazing," he would insist, "and little attention." In the end the reluctant student would be confronted with how little his or her visual memory had retained. One describes his experience of being assigned to observe a Persian rug.

> In the end we were forced to study our objects down to the last detail, and to describe them. In my case, I was called on five times before I succeeded. This work at high pressure lasted half an hour. Our eyes were tired and our attention strained.... [After a break] the time [given for] observation was cut down from thirty seconds to twenty. The Assistant Director remarked that the allowance for observation would eventually be reduced to two seconds.[10]

Viola Spolin agrees with Stanislavski about the importance of seeing. Not only do such exercises develop concentration and observation skills; but authentic seeing enables authentic listening, which, in turn, makes authentic relationships possible. Staring is not seeing, she reminds her students:

> Staring is a curtain in front of the eyes as surely as though the eyes were closed. It is a mirror reflecting the actor to himself. It is isolation. Student-actors who *stare* but do not see prevent themselves from directly experiencing their environment and entering into relationships.[11]

Another popular way of building the concentration "muscle" is practiced by actors working together in pairs.[12] An ability to balance relaxation and kinesthetic focus, and at the same time gain access to the unconscious is the payoff for the famous "mirrors" exercise. Two actors face each other, standing in the base position, several inches apart. One actor initiates a slow movement which the other follows, as if in a mirror. Eye contact is maintained. There is no touching and no talking. The movement is continuous. The initiator juggles three priorities: respect for the other person's physical limits, freshness and originality in movement, and achievement of a beyond-thinking state of being where the body seems to take over and movement is directed by something beyond thought. The mirrorer aims for accuracy in the reproduction of the movement, relaxation and achievement of a beyond-thinking state.

When the exercise works well, an altered state is produced for both initiator and mirrorer that may be described as a state of deepened concentration. The consistent practice of such an exercise over a period of years is said to build a person's capacity for concentration as well as her or his facility in gaining access to that desirable state.

Many artists say they find the rhythmic movement of such an exercise and repetitive movement in general helpful in reaching a deeper state of concentration. (Yoga is an example of another popular method that utilizes this insight to deepen relaxation and heighten concentration.) Preachers may notice the importance of repetitive movement in the more ordinary aspects of daily life—not only does the rhythmic motion of the car put baby to sleep, it facilitates some of our best sermon ideas. Cooking (especially kneading, chopping, dicing, and paring), driving, and showering all involve repetitive, regular movement. All of them may facilitate deeper concentration and prime the pump to that great reservoir of creativity, the unconscious.

Other concentration exercises may be done individually. They are listed here in the form prescribed by M. A. Chekov, who worked in the Second Moscow Art Theatre Studio under Stanislavski.

1. Study the wall paper pattern so that you can describe it and reproduce it accurately.
2. Listen to a sound.
3. Do an arithmetic problem in your head.
4. Select and follow a single sound out of a confusion of noise.
5. Do several activities in succession: look at the pictures in a magazine, listen to music, dance, do arithmetic problems. Then turn rapidly from one activity to the next, making sure that the transference of attention each time is complete and genuine.
6. Note, in a few seconds, as many details as possible of someone's clothes.
7. Concentrate upon an idea or problem. (Have) five or six people ask questions that must be answered without having the attention waver from this idea.
8. Master the contents of a book while others talk.
9. Concentrate on a tune in your head while other music is being played.[13]

❧ OBSERVATION ❧

An actor should be observant not only on the stage, but also in real life. He should concentrate with all his being on whatever attracts his attention. He should look at an object, not as any absent-minded passerby, but with penetration. Otherwise his whole creative method will prove lopsided and bear no relation to life.[14]

WE MUST WORK ON VISUALIZATION & MEMORY

One of the simplest concentration/observation exercises is also one of the most challenging: the memorization of a tree. A friend, a long-time actor and director, describes his practice of the exercise. Each day on the way to and from his office, he says, he passes the same tree and is able to observe it at some length. His goal is to memorize its shape and branches, to be able to call up an accurate mental picture of it when he is not within sight of it. He works methodically through the tree, noticing and memorizing its shape. He has been about the business of memorizing this tree for twenty years. "Nobody sees a flower—really—it is so small and it takes time—we haven't time—and to see takes time, like to have a

What Actors Know

friend takes time," says Georgia O'Keefe.[15] But she is wrong about my friend.

Actors find that one of the most effective ways to sharpen one's observation skills is by observing nature.

> Nothing in life is more beautiful than nature, and it should be the object of constant observation. To begin with, take a little flower, or a petal from it, or a spider web, or a design made by frost on the window pane. Try to express in words what it is in these things that gives pleasure.[16]

Such sharpening of observation skills helps not only to develop a person's ability to concentrate, but provides the artist with the raw materials for creative work. Sights, sounds, smells, experiences, and especially images that are closely observed are stored in the artist's memory banks as fuel for the creative process.

> Art is an image-using system. In order to create, we draw from our inner well . . . if we don't give attention to upkeep, our well is apt to become depleted, stagnant or blocked. . . . Filling the well involves the active pursuit of images to refresh our artistic reservoirs. Art is born in attention. Its midwife is detail.[17]

Many of the concentration exercises listed above also build observation skills. These three additional exercises aim specifically at improving the preacher's powers of observation:

ADD DESCRIPTORS

1. *Narrative detail.* Improvise orally or write, in five or six sentences, a bare-bones description of a recent incident in your own life. Use nouns and verbs, but no adjectives or adverbs. For example, "I was walking down the street when someone in a passing car waved. The car pulled over, and a friend of mine got out. While we were talking, a dog came down the sidewalk and sniffed our shoes. Just as I put my hand down to pet the dog, it trotted off. I frowned after it, as my friend laughed."

Next rewrite the story adding color to each sentence. For example, "I was walking down a gray street when someone in a passing car waved. The bright red car pulled over, and a friend of mine got out. While we were talking, a black dog came down the sidewalk and sniffed our brown shoes. Just as I put my flesh-colored hand down to pet the dog, it trotted off. I frowned darkly after it, as my friend laughed."

The exercise may be repeated adding visual, aural, olfactory, and texture details in turn. If the exercise is to be done in a group setting, it may be practiced using the method of Viola Spolin. Spolin recommends a similar exercise where two people cooperate in relating an incident. One tells the story first in its bare bones form, and the other repeats the story adding color.[18] Whichever form the exercise takes, the object is not to compose great prose but to stretch one's muscles of observation.

*2. *Timed walk*   Take a twenty-minute walk, absorbing every instance of pink. At the end of the walk, replay in your mind, write brief sketches, or relate orally to a friend everything you observed that was pink. HOW MUCH PINK IS ON MY 20 MINUTE WALK? HOW MUCH CAN I RECALL?

3. Widening apertures   Buy a roll of film and shoot the whole roll in one solitary walk. If your camera allows, experiment with distances and lighting options.

••• IMAGINATION •••

The creation of a character by an actor is an act of imagination. The creation of a sermon is too. Imagination does not, of course, invent God, as Garrett Green and others have shown. It is more the case that the Holy Spirit establishes a point of contact in the matrix of human imagination, habilitating the ability given to us at creation.

If sermons are, as we have said, more than a serial restatement of a text's main ideas,[19] where do the non-biblical words come from? What inspires those connections that cause the sermon to take wing and fly? What puts flesh on the bones exegesis digs up? Mental pictures. While logic, deductive reasoning, linear thought, and argument have their place in preaching, it is a much smaller place than it once was. Contemporary preachers have discovered that linear rationality alone makes for a pretty dead sermon. What does it take to give a sermon life? It takes human life—conjured by imagination, transfused by empathy, and conveyed in mental pictures.

"Imagination consists in associating known objects, uniting, separating, modifying, recombining them."[20] It is, in short, the artist's instrument of discovery. Effective sermons use imaginative ability to bring the text to life, with integrity and reverence, for a specific time and place. They discover the means for accomplishing this end by associating, combining, and recombining aspects of the known and the unknown.

In more general terms, imagination may be described as the door to creativity. It is, at once, creativity's catalytic agent and its channel, spark, and conductor.[21] In the interpretative arts, imagination often flows, as the word itself suggests, from images. We might say it flows from, in, around, through images. In addition, image is the language form most closely associated with emotion. So it is in the arranging and rearranging of images[22] that imagination is invoked and emotions are stirred.

In theatre, imagination is the first half of an actor's creative task, the half that unleashes emotion. Imagination is made possible by something Stanislavski called "The Magic If." The word *if* is magical, he believed, because it gives us permission to be something other than what we are. To teach his students this, Stanislavski might place a ball in their midst, asking them to respond to it as if it were a poisonous snake. The next moment he might ask them to imagine that it was a human infant, a cake, or a basket of eggs. He would then point out the contrasts between their various reactions to the object, teasing out of the student actors a recognition of the emotions that lay behind them.

Though the actors were never told to feel fear or tenderness, they experienced those feelings in response to a particular image—an image largely created by their imaginations. Similarly, in interpreting a script, if an actor can "enter" the imaginary circumstances of the play by way of her or his imagination, and then follow the play's action (i.e., via motivating images)[23] through its course, it is believed that the appropriate emotions will flow and inspiration will come.

There is no reason to believe that the use of imagination cannot work in a similar way for preachers. The process cannot be very much different for them, though it is circumscribed by exegesis' findings and hermeneutic's decisions. Actors are bound by similar parameters—research into character and the director's interpretation of the text, for example. If Stanislavski's disciplined use of imagination can provide actors with such reliable results, there is every reason to believe that preachers will find it useful.

If the preacher is able to enter the circumstances of the biblical text by way of imagination and then carefully follow the unfolding action of the text (i.e., from motivating image to motivating image) appropriate emotions will emerge and connections will be made. For the preacher's creative process, the role of imagination is no less important than it is for the actor's. Fortunately, the key that unlocks emotion and inspiration is available to both.

Almost anything that involves following, associating, or juxtaposing mental pictures can exercise the imagination. However, there are a few classic exercises the preacher may wish to adapt for his or her use.

I LOVE THE EXERCISES NOT JUST THEORY.

1. *Writing off the page.*[24]   The only rules in the "writing off the page" exercise are that you keep your hand moving across the page and you do it for a prescribed time. That's right, your hand. No keyboards. Pen or pencil and paper are used for this exercise. Set yourself a goal in terms of time (ten, fifteen, or twenty minutes) or pages (two or three) and keep your hand moving until you reach that goal. It is perfectly fine to write "I don't know what to write" over and over until something else comes.

Focus on a strong image—something that has emotional power for you. See it on your mental motion picture screen. Clear your mind of distractions until you are able to follow the unfolding of that mental picture. Begin writing, just following the image. Let feelings emerge. Allow the mental scene to unfold as it will. The picture may move, other images may enter the scene, a story may or may not begin to form. The only responsibilities you have are to follow the image and to keep your hand moving.

2. Musical pictures.   Write or improvise out loud the images called up by your favorite piece of instrumental music. Keep it concrete. "This makes me feel happy" is an abstraction. Say what you see instead. "I see yellow spinning wheels. They seem to be made of fire." Encourage yourself to create fantastic pictures. Allow your body's responses to feed the developing imagery.

3. Animals and people.   Look for resemblances between animals or objects and people or experiment with portraying ideas as animals or objects.[25] Write a paragraph or tell a friend about a person you know well, portraying that person as a drinking fountain or an unbroken colt, for example. Develop the habit of associating people with animals or objects.   WHAT ANIMAL WOULD CROW BE?

Concentration, observation, and imagination twine together to undergird the preacher's creative process. The power of imagery and rhythm combine with the kind of psycho-physical disciplines described above to unlock the resources of the preacher's unconscious. The good news is that the skills involved require abilities that are inborn and accessible and that, like muscles, may be improved with exercise. The less-happy news is that they do not develop automatically. For the committed artist and the passionate preacher, they represent disciplines that are practiced over the course of a lifetime.

••• A CERTAIN ETHOS •••

Theatre is more than the disciplined practice of a particular craft. Behind the mechanics and skills that bring theatre into being, there are the norms and values that shape its ethos. These habitus, or habits of the heart and hand, are strategically important in making the collaborative aspect of theatre work and in making it "art." While they may vary tremendously from troupe to troupe, company to company, and school to school, it is possible to generalize about a few of the attitudes actors hold in common and that may be seen to comprise the heart or soul of the theatre. The purpose of this exploration is merely heuristic. It is hoped that a conversation between actors and preachers on this subject may stimulate further discussion in the church about the attitudes and values that underlie its worship.

HABITUS #1: A COMMITMENT TO ENERGY

Acting is fundamentally a matter of being able to "live" on stage. As drama critic Eric Bentley put it, "The actor's fundamental contribution is not mimicry but vitality...[the actor's purpose] is to give off life, to make it audible and visible."[26] A good actor is an actor who brings life onto the stage with her. It is the main thing an actor owes a playwright, call it presence, vitality, projection, energy, or life. Artistic actors make a commitment to bring a certain level of energy to their work.

Life is manifested in the performance of a play in many different ways. Certainly, there is no one way life's electricity or juice or sap comes to the stage, anymore than there is just one way life may come into the pulpit. It may be noticeable in an actor's vocal intensity or on a preacher's cheeks. We may sense it in the bend of an elbow or the extension of an arm. It may be seen in a flash of teeth or in the long strides that carry the preacher the length of the chancel. When it is present, the people in the pew or the mezzanine seats may not think about it at all; but they are guaranteed to notice its absence.

Perhaps if it could be said that if there is any one way of "living" on stage that is indispensable, that way would have something to do with the meeting of eyes.

> The meeting of the eyes constitutes a kind of center of human communication. The contact established is more personal than touch. What is communicated may be in doubt, but what is not in doubt is the aliveness of the lines of communication....Usually when we speak of seeing something through another's eyes, we are speaking only of the mind's eye. In the theatre, the actors' eyes guide us through the labyrinthine ways of the scenes; and all that joins us to the actors' eyes is the magnetics of looking. In the theatre, we may not be led by the nose: we are led by the eyes.[27]

If the locus of electricity in theatre is the meeting of the actors' eyes—if we are, as Bentley says, "led by the eyes" of the actors—

what leads us in preaching? How is it that the dramatic action of the text is embodied? Bentley's insight suggests that a key source of electricity in the preaching moment is in the meeting of the preacher's eyes and the eyes of the congregation.

Although there is only one actor on stage Sunday morning at eleven o'clock, that does not mean she has no one to "play" with her. All that is said about the power of actors' eyes may be said about preachers'—they create a center of communication, the contact established is more personal than touch, and they "guide" the action. What actors do indirectly, preachers do directly. Both depend upon the electricity generated by eye contact.

Obviously, the importance of eye contact in preaching argues strongly for the kind of sermon delivery that is "freed from the manuscript." But whether a preacher appears in the pulpit noteless, with an outline, or with a full manuscript, eye contact is not to be taken for granted. The harnessing and orchestration of eye contact's power in preaching requires a certain intentionality. Key phrases that deserve the kind of underlining effect the eye can give must be identified and should be rehearsed. Other passages that are more appropriately interpreted with indirect eye focus will also need rehearsal.[28]

Few preachers can assume that the eye contact that comes to them "naturally" (by which is often meant "without thought or preparation") will be the most effective. Preachers who use manuscripts tend to fall into marked patterns that can be distracting and that send a strong nonverbal message. The message may be "I don't care that you know that I'm reading this," "I'm nervous" or "This is all routine to me." But it is never a positive message.

Perhaps the most common of these patterns is that of looking at the congregation near the beginning of each sentence, then down at the page for the last few words. If a preacher can do nothing else in the area of eye contact, he or she owes it to the congregation to do at least this much: break the habit involved in this pattern. This may be achieved by forcing oneself to take in the last of a sentence in a glance and willing oneself to maintain eye contact until one reaches the period.

Of course those who preach with only brief notes or outlines are not exempt from having eye contact problems. They often bring with them manuscript habits (learned from previous experience with manuscripts or from observing manuscript preachers), looking down at the lectern even when no note is there. Even those who take only mental notes with them into the pulpit do not always make intentional use of the power of eye contact. Most preachers who stand behind a pulpit have at some time or other sought its protection. There are times when it is more comfortable to make eye contact with an oak slab than with a live elder. Everybody needs a refuge sometimes, but to choose comfort over connection too often may endanger the very life of the sermon.

It is the task of both preachers and actors to bring life to the stage. They must break every habit that stymies them in meeting this goal, use every means at their disposal to accomplish it, and constantly be seeking new means. Arthur Hopkins put it more picturesquely nearly a century ago:

> Have nothing to do with morgues or graveyards. Keep alive and awake and insistent and enthusiastic and forever ready to knock the first head that shows in the wrong alley and grab any hand that shows in the right one.[29]

HABITUS #2: A RESPECT FOR THE BODY

Just as it is necessary to still the conscious mind in order for the artist to tap the resources of the unconscious, it is necessary for the performer—actor or preacher—to still the conscious mind of the audience in order to reach audience members at the unconscious level. The unconscious minds of audience members are "stilled" by the elimination of physical distraction. For this reason Arthur Hopkins states:

> I eliminate all gesture that is not absolutely needed, all unnecessary inflections and intonings, the tossing of heads, the flickering of fans and kerchiefs, the tapping of feet, drumming of fingers, swinging of legs, pressing of brows, holding of hearts, curling of moustaches, stroking of beards, and all the million and one tricks that have crept into the actor's bag, all of them betraying one of two things—an

annoying lack of repose, or an attempt to attract attention to himself and away from the play.[30]

In order to achieve this kind of streamlining of movement, actors cultivate their ability to move with economy and purpose and strive to set aside habitual gestures. The goal is to create of the body a kind of clean slate—if not a tabula rasa—on which the text (the play's lines, the words of the scriptural text, the moves of the sermon) can express itself. Said another way, a good actor aims to create of her body a sensitive instrument, an instrument that is ready to respond to the smallest signal and that is unimpeded by the clutter of nervous or idiosyncratic gestures.

When this goal is achieved, the actor is "stripped" of distracting mannerisms and freed to move with purpose. Twin goals govern the actor's use of the body. First, "Every movement on the stage should mean something."[31] And, second, the actor must find the easiest way to accomplish the task. Again, purposeful, economic movement is the goal. Since strain calls attention to itself, it is a distraction that breaks the spell. It is as problematic in this regard as excess movement. Both are to be avoided. Instead, the actor "must think of the play as a clean ball. Whenever it is tossed to him he should pass it on without smearing it with his perspiration."[32]

Fundamental to the tasks of "stripping" and training oneself to move with purpose and economy is a healthy appreciation for the body. Well-trained actors value and respect the human body as the potentially powerful instrument of expression it is. It is out of this sense of respect that they cultivate body-awareness and let down some of the inhibitions about the body that most people carry. An actor who is kinesthetically sensitive, whose movement has been pruned, and who experiences a healthy sense of freedom about her or his body, is more "available" to the play and more likely to be effective in embodying its movement.

Preachers too need to make their bodies available to the sermon's movement. Whether they pace the length of the chancel and the center aisle or stand behind a chin-high panel, it is dangerous for preachers to treat their bodies casually—or, worse, to let a negative view of the body impede embodiment. In the former case, we

115

are likely to succumb to the temptation to use the kind of excess movement that breaks the spell we are aiming to cast, and in the latter we risk reinforcing in the congregation the old dualistic notion that sees the flesh as evil.

Traditionally, preachers and their congregations have shown an amazing ability to avoid the question about the body's use in preaching. One way this is done in many congregations is to treat the spoken word as if it were purely the head's invention.

> We tend to think of (words) as springing from somewhere around the neck up. That is to say we are curiously unaware of their physical nature, and think of them mainly in terms of expressing reasons and ideas and of colouring them with feelings, and not in terms of our physical being expressed through them and involved in them.[33]

But words, even the most high-flown sacred words, derive from the body as well as from cerebral processes. Language started, after all, with the grunts, vocalized nudges and mouth-noises needed to signal distress or need and "mere words" still have the power to "hit us at gut level." We may be more comfortable thinking about language as a sophisticated signal system—and it is. But it is at the same time a primitive system—a system that derives from and resonates in the body. If "The Word was made flesh and dwelt among us" implies anything about the nature of preaching, it suggests that preachers will have come to terms with the physical side of those phonemes that Broca's area so neatly manufactures and pushes out of their mouths.

Of course the more of the preacher's body that is visible to the congregation, the more important is its use in preaching and the more important respect for the body is. However, there are few contemporary preachers who are not being pressed to "come out from the pulpit" more. As congregational expectations about and general appreciation for the importance of visual communication continue to increase, fewer and fewer preachers will find it satisfying or effective to limit their nonverbal range to head and eye movement.

116

Habitus #3: Hospitality

Of all the habits of hand and heart that are practiced by theatre artists, the habit of hospitality may be the most important. A good theatre invites the audience members in and makes them comfortable. It anticipates their every need—help finding a seat, a program to orient them to the production, an intermission to accommodate their physical needs—and tries to make being at the play as easy as it can possibly be. Of course, the theatre is motivated by commercial concerns. It certainly is in the theatre's best interests to remove every obstacle between the box office and the consumer's dollar. However, the interesting thing is that what began in self-interest has evolved into a wider concern. Hospitality has become a hallmark of the art of theatre. Many actors practice it with a particular kind of pride. The theatre traditionally extends hospitality like nobody else—not even the church.

There are three aspects of the theatre's practice of hospitality that are potentially useful to the preacher: attention to comfort, accessibility and audience presence.

Comfort

Just think in stereotypic terms for a moment. Why do you suppose it is that pews are hard and theatre seats are cushiony, sanctuaries are always too hot or too cold and theatres are climate-controlled, chancels are drab and sets are visually stimulating? Why are you more likely to see a troupe of earnest young actors sweeping their space and almost-lovingly arranging the chairs on Saturday afternoon than you are to see a preacher picking up last week's bulletins? Why do theatres work so hard to make parking available and tickets easy to buy while the church usher ostentatiously sticks the plate under your nose as you arrive late—breathless from the long walk in from the car?

Oh, you protest, there are many churches that are comfortable and many theatres that are forbidding. Yes, but remember we are just thinking in generalizations for the moment. Why, in general, is the comfort of the audience more of a priority for the commercial theatre than it is for the church of Jesus Christ?

Money, of course, as we have already said, is one possible explanation. A theatre that does not make attendance comfortable risks losing income. The church is less concerned about money than theatre, we say, and that is the way we want it. Or we may hypothesize that the church has traditionally had the same kind of mixed feelings about beauty and physical comfort as it has had about the body. Or we may say that it relies on a sense of duty or commitment to bring its members to worship. There are many ways to explain how it is (in the instances when it is) that the church is less hospitable than the theatre. The explanations might be more than enough to keep churches from ever having to raise questions about the congregation's comfort—if it weren't for the fact that so many of them are so empty.

In many theatres, actors, directors, and crew take a kind of loving pride in the welcoming environment they create for the evening's guests. In some houses, these acts of thoughtfulness and hospitality come near to being an offering to the "glory of the theatre." Should those who work in God's house and serve God's glory be less attentive to the needs of those who come to worship?

ACCESSIBILITY

"Never turn your back on the audience." It is perhaps the most widely known dictum from actors' training. The ability of the audience to see and hear, to maintain visual and aural contact with the actors, is a priority in the theatre. While this may occasionally mean that actors' backs are an issue, it mostly means that acoustics and sightlines are carefully monitored. The goal is to make the audience's seeing and hearing effortless, to remove every obstacle or impediment. If that means that for certain stage designs, the seats in certain sections of the house have an obscured view of the stage, then those seats are roped off. If it means that body mikes have to be added to an intimate scene, they are added. The actors, director, and crew take responsibility for the ability of the audience to see and hear the play.

While many churches have been working conscientiously on acoustics, most have not given as much consideration to sightlines.

On a given Sunday morning in most mainline churches across the country, there will be at least seven minutes out of sixty when no one in the congregation who is sitting farther back than the first pew will be able to see what is going on in the chancel. Often they will miss all or part of what is said as well. When it is time for the "children's sermon," it is time for the people left sitting in the pews to choose. They may either strain their eyes and crane their necks or settle back and hope to be able to overhear the preacher's words. A commitment on the part of the church to make it possible for everybody to see and hear everything would go a long way, not only in making worship more welcoming, but in making it more inclusive.

THE PRESENCE OF THE AUDIENCE

If there is an actor's dictum that is more widely known outside the theatre than "never turn your back on the audience," it is the famous line—often delivered in majestic (and sometimes manic) tones—"The show must go on!" Why must the show go on? Why is it so important in the theatre that the turned ankle of the ingenue or the laryngitis of the lead tenor not be allowed to delay the opening curtain?

There are a number of ways to answer the question. The show must go on out of respect for the people who have managed to get to their seats by eight o'clock. The show must go on because there are so many more of them than there are of us and they are the paying customers. The show must go on because the person-hours that all those full seats represent so outweigh the person-hours that the ingenue or the tenor—or, indeed, the whole cast—has invested in this evening. The show must go on because the audience is ready and they are the reason for the play.

The show goes on in the theatre, despite the inconvenience of the actors, as the ultimate act of hospitality. Just as a woman who throws a dinner party would not dream of leaving her guests cooling their heels while she runs upstairs to apply a third coat of mascara or to feed the cat, so no theatre worth its salt would make an audience wait while the conductor looks for his favorite baton. On the contrary, the music cues are picked up in a heartbeat. The baton rises as the last word fades from the actor's lips. There are no gaps. The play marches forward with everyone on stage making the supreme effort to avoid being the one to drop the ball. Why? To make the actors appear more professional? Because there is something pleasing about an uninterrupted flow of words? In order to discourage people from leaving the theatre early? No. These things are a result of a profound respect. Equal, or nearly equal, to the respect an actor holds for the text is the respect an actor holds for the audience's presence—a respect that is held at the front of the actors' minds for so long that it becomes an ingrained way of thinking. It becomes a habit to regard the interests of others as superseding your own. It becomes a habit of heart and hand to extend hospitality to the stranger, in hopes of making a friend.

Chapter Six

Worship as Theatre

"Surely this is what it should look like," I thought to myself, "when the people of God bring their tithes into God's storehouse." What it looked like was a stream of brightly colored heavenly host. Chartreuse, hot pink, yellow, and electric blue poured down the aisle as the music swelled. The dresses flowed. Chiffon swirled between charcoal gray and navy blue wool shoulders. The colors eddied and flowed forward together, pooling finally around the bottom step of the platform as the pastor walked out to accept the offering.

There were dozens of them, maybe scores. Men in business suits and women in Korean traditional dress who had collected the large crowd's offerings in buckets, now crowded eagerly at the edge of the chancel to present them. There was the kind of crackle in the air that only happens when several thousand people have reached for their wallets and gotten to their feet. The Mass Choir off to my left was truly a mass. Hundreds of young Korean men and women sang in what sounded to me like the heavenly language spoken in the Pentecostal church of my youth. The drums were loud and the violins insistent. From my place in the front row, I sang along to the familiar melody in English, unworried that anyone would be distracted—or, indeed, that anyone would hear me.

We were all standing nicely in our places, yet feeling the pull of the crowd forward. Led by our eyes, we surged gently with the ushers as the pastor's hands reached down to take the offering buckets. We could see the corners of bills peeking over their tops. I imagined the coins at the bottom.

Several verses went by. I began to anticipate the moment when the processional would be reversed and the chiffon would flow back up the aisle, but the church knew better than that. As we reached the last chorus, the men and women filed quietly out doors on either side of the chancel, the lights dimmed slightly, and the pastor appeared in the pulpit.

It could have been the Pentecostal church of my youth or a mid-century Presbyterian church, perhaps in the Great Plains region of the United States. It could have been one of the hundreds of revival services my grandmother attended during her youth, held in dusty tents in the small towns of southern California. But it wasn't. It was Seoul, Korea, and it was nearly the end of the twentieth century.

It was certainly an old-fashioned style of worship—reflecting the legacy of those earnest young westerners who helped plant the Presbyterian church in Korea more than a century ago. It was simple and familiar. It was not novel, it was not contemporary, it was not something new and fresh. But it was energetic. It was careful. It was full of grace and it was full of truth. There was balance and there was life. Both the Fall and the Redemption were accounted for. People were offered a chance to open themselves to God. There were moments of illumination. Most of all, it moved.

It was worship and it was theatre. The Scripture was opened. Thousands of human hearts lifted. The Spirit of God moved through the room. And the alms overflowed their buckets.

✦✦✦ WORSHIP AS THEATRE ✦✦✦

Once one begins to see resonance between the disciplines of preaching and theatre, it is not difficult to imagine the parallels between worship and theatre. Indeed Søren Kierkegaard already has. Kierkegaard, of course, was an avid theatre-goer. It is said that, "he spent most of his life's evenings in the Royal Theater, and he was more frequently in the theater than in the church."[1] So it is not particularly surprising that his famous reconceptualization of worship's roles draws on theatrical sensibilities. What is surprising about Kierkegaard's model derives from the angle of his viewing. Instead of paralleling preachers and actors, audiences and congregations, Kierkegaard wrinkled the schema. He pictured the congregation on stage as the actors playing to God in the audience—with the preacher prompting from the wings.[2]

It is appropriate to begin an examination of worship and theatre with such a reminder. What is valuable about this exercise—about paralleling the act of worship with the act of theatre—is not the straight lines we may draw, not the roles we match up, but the insight into the nature of worship that stands to be gained from the comparison. Kierkegaard reminds us that worship is never about what it looks like it's about. The parallels seem so obvious. Each involves a stage and a smaller group of people facing a larger group of people. Each revolves around the interpretation of texts. Both are corporate, artistic events. In addition, there is much to be gained from a comparison between the actor's skills and values and those of the preacher, as we have seen. It becomes nearly irresistible to begin thinking about delivering a product to the people sitting in the pews.

Ultimately, though, worship can never be about actors on a stage performing for other people. Even the high view of *theatre, actor* and *performance* we have been exploring here cannot make a case for that. Worship is about *all* of God's people performing—giving form to[3]—their response to God. Whether leaders and congregation play together in the middle of the cosmic stage or whether it is, as Kierkegaard would have it, more appropriate to push the preacher off to the side a bit and into the wings, worship is something that the people of God do together and something that they do for God. While the final form of a play may be pictured hovering like a ghost somewhere around the proscenium arch as the words of the last line die away, the final form of worship hovers over the middle of the nave. A theatre critic's bottom line has to do with what the playwright, director, crew, and actors achieve; but if there were such creatures as "worship critics," they would care only about what happens to the congregants.

The chief difference between theatre and worship is a strategic one, though it may amount to a difference of emphasis. The theatre cares about the viewers' experience, but "the play's the thing." Worship cares about the liturgy, but the participants' participation is paramount. Theatre cannot be worship, except perhaps under one special, and probably rare, condition—when it is offered up to God by both the actors and the audience. Some passion plays may achieve this, for example. Some theatre companies where the members are people of faith may aim for this. But as a rule, theatre is not worship. It is possible to say, though, that under certain circumstances, worship can be theatre.

Worship and theatre have a great deal in common. To begin with, they have the same things in common that we have already noticed about preaching and theatre or about preaching and art: they create an experience with drawing power and open viewers' apertures, facilitating discovery, encounter, and even transformation. But worship and theatre share even more ground than preaching and theatre. In fact, the strategically important aspect of worship—the aspect which Kierkegaard is at pains to remind us about—is the very thing that is distinctive about theatre: worship and theatre are collaborative acts.

It is from collaborative activity that the peculiar kind of life that is characteristic of worship and artful theatre arises. Out of identification and empathy, in the meeting of eyes and the interchange of voices, in communal response to image, a synergy is born and community is achieved. Arthur Hopkins shows the importance of synergy and community in theatre, stating the case in the extreme. "The theatre is always seeking unanimous reaction," he says. "Twelve people will solve a problem twelve different ways, but five thousand will respond to a note struck unanimously."[4] The church too is seeking a kind of unanimous reaction. Not, perhaps, at the level of thought, but at the level of spiritual experience; a moment of unanimous reaction can be life-giving. When five thousand people are galvanized by the striking of one note—or by the offering of a sermon's image—an energy is generated. When five hundred people "talk back" to the preacher, as happens in the African American church, a live circuit is created. When five people with linked hands listen to the sound of one voice praying, community is born. "Where two or three agree together as touching any one thing...."

When worship is also theatre it effects a lively communion that is more than communication. Communication is about transmitting information or passing along a message. The word carries with it a sense of transportation through space. Communion has more to do with the energy that establishes and maintains relationships in time.[5] "Communion is an ambience that draws beings together in a circle of energy through a common act or shared experience at a level of inwardness."[6] It is from this energy—the energy that draws the circle together—the energy of The Annunciator—that worship derives its life.

✦✦✦ THEATRE VERSUS RITUAL ✦✦✦

Kierkegaard was not the first to be interested in the parallels and twists by which theatre and worship may be compared. The definitive study of worship and theatre was done in 1965 by O. B. Hardison, Jr. In *Christian Rite and Christian Drama in the Middle Ages,* Hardison examines the shape of the Mass during the golden age of church-and-theatre relations. He concludes that the medieval Mass in certain times and places was "sacred drama." Hardison agrees with other historians that the understanding of secular drama during the High Middle Ages was quite elementary. However he observes that Honorius of Artun's twelfth-century view of the Mass indicates that some people of this time were able not only to see the Mass as theatre but to appreciate the orchestration of its various elements.

> Honorius not only uses the vocabulary of dramatic criticism, he uses it with considerable sophistication. The church is regarded as theater. The drama enacted has a coherent plot based on conflict (duellum) between a champion and an antagonist. The plot has a rising action, culminating in the Passion and entombment. At its climax there is a dramatic reversal, the Resurrection, correlated

with the emotional transition from the Canon of the Mass to Communion.[7]

For many, Hardison's work stands as the last word on the dramatic nature of the Mass during the key period of the Middle Ages. However, Richard Schechner, an early voice in the growing Performance Studies movement, has questioned the appropriateness of equating the worship of the church with theatre. In Schechner's lexicon, the appropriate comparison lies between worship and "ritual." The root of the difference is that Schechner and others from the social sciences' approach to theatre (see, for example, Victor Turner, *From Ritual to Theatre*) define theatre's purpose as "entertainment" and understand ritual in terms of "efficacy."[8] Theatre, Schechner believes, arises out of a separation between actors and audience. It is important to Schechner's understanding of theatre that the audience has the right to attend or to refuse to attend. They make the decision to attend or not based on their desire to be entertained and the perceived potential for the fulfillment of that desire. Because the Mass had a hold on the participants, because they were obliged to be there, and because they were chiefly interested in its spiritual effects, Schechner insists, "the Mass was not theatre in its classic or modern sense."[9]

It should be obvious to the reader already that the use of the term *theatre* in this study has more in common with Hardison's than Schechner's. A broader definition of *theatre* than that used by Schechner is employed here. Indeed, the definition of *theatre* used here has much in common with Schechner's *ritual*.

I see theatre as a collaborative art form in which players and audience willingly participate and which has the capacity to open us to discovery, illumination, and ultimately, transformation; *and* I believe that the agenda of theatre, understood this way, bears a striking similarity to worship's agenda. I am interested in drawing parallels between theatre and worship, not only for the sake of the practical implications—for the observations about actors' skills, etc., which may be useful to worship leaders—but because, among all the art forms, it is *theatre* in which we find the mirror of action and the potential for incarnational activity—for enlivened, embodied performance. These concerns are also worship's concerns. More than that, they speak to an area of contemporary church life where there is a need and a lack.

It should be clear too that I am speaking of a different church situation from that of the medieval church which Schechner describes. While it may be the case that church attendance during the High Middle Ages was obligatory, it is hardly the case today. Today, worship leaders—especially worship leaders of the mainline Protestant churches—are in a situation more like classic and modern actors', hoping to find an audience for their work. So even in Schechner's specialized definition of *theatre*, the church of today and the theatre have much in common.

In chapter 2 we explored three aspects of performance art that apply to both theatre and preaching and that may be seen to account for the semblance of life in each. These same aspects—action, distance, and performance—will be helpful here in showing something about the source of liveliness, of life, in the worship of the church.

✦✦✦ WORSHIP AND ACTION ✦✦✦

Dramatic action and literal action are as important to worship as they are to theatre and preaching. Dramatic action springs from conflict and creates the suspense or momentum in a worship service, which both draws the participant into the worship experience and carries her through it. From the actor's point of view it is this "spine" of the play, or aspects of it, that he or she renders in what Stanislavski called "the unbroken line."

> On the stage, if the inner line is broken an actor no longer understands what is being said or done.... The actor and the part, humanly speaking, live by these unbroken lines. *That is what gives life and movement to what is being enacted.*[10]

The term *dramatic action* is used to designate the impetus behind the play or worship service's events and physical activity, not the deeds themselves.[11] Without a strong line of dramatic action, a worship service feels erratic, flat, or dead.

Literal or physical action in a worship service is comprised of the movements the participants make. Both large movements that carry a person down the aisle, across the chancel, or up the steps into the pulpit and small movements that break bread, pour wine, and sprinkle water comprise the service's literal or physical action. Physical action may also be useful as a kind of indicator of the strength of the dramatic action—an outward manifestation of the "healthiness" of the through line which propels the service. In addition, physical action, carelessly handled, can sabotage even a strong line of dramatic action. Ideally, the two reinforce each other.

➤➤➤ THE WORSHIP SERVICE AND PLOT ➤➤➤

In the theatre, strong dramatic action is manifested in strong plot. For a worship service too, plot is important. Since Aristotle, plot has been understood as the "arrangement of the incidents"[12] by which the action of the play is expressed. In simple story or plain narrative, incidents are merely strung together with *and*s or, at most, arranged in chronological order. However, the word *plot* implies something more. Minimally, Aristotle says, it implies "a beginning, a middle and an end."[13]

Plot is narrative with "something done to it; the rearrangement of incidents in the order calculated to have the right effect."[14] The "something done to it" may be as simple as the addition of causality. As E. M. Forster says, "The king died and then the queen died is a story, but it becomes a plot if we write: The king died and then the queen died of grief."[15] Most often, plot is a result of selecting certain incidents and arranging them to show cause and effect. A well-conceived plot reaches toward the maximum sensation of movement.

While there are a number of ways to talk about the principles that guide the arranging of incidents, the most familiar categories—conflict, rising action, climax (or reversal), and denouement (or resolution)—are, perhaps, most useful for considering the place of dramatic action or plot in worship.

CONFLICT: Worship opens with conflict on one or a number of levels. In theatre, conflict is often established by an inciting incident that leads to a dramatic question around which the play is organized. The question shapes the action of the play. For example, in Sophocles' *Oedipus the King,* Oedipus asks the oracle at Delphi for help in ending a plague.[16] The oracle answers that King Laius' murderer must be found. Immediately, the conflict is established (finding the murderer versus not finding the murderer), the question is raised (will the murderer by found?), and the play is off and running. The action is set in motion.

Worship, however, requires no specific incident to prompt the congregation to question or to set the service in motion. The congregation comes to worship each and every week in the midst of any number of conflicts. It is the purpose of the worship service to play out a conflict in a way that makes it possible for the congregation to see God's presence in it. In any given week, the conflict at play may be drawn from aspects of the cosmic drama of fall and redemption or from ordinary life. While a service of worship does not require an inciting incident, it does require that the planner choose and focus the conflict.

The worship service answers the questions these conflicts pose— from "Am I saved or am I damned?" to "Where is hope to be found?" Such themes may be focused and expressed in preparation for worship, the call to worship, opening hymns, music, and/or opening prayers. This conflict gives rise to the service's dramatic action. Possible themes include

- conflict between who God is and whom we know ourselves to be (between our need for union with God and our alienation from God)
- conflict between our desire to adore God and our need to confess
- conflict between the claim of God on our lives and the pull of the daily world
- conflict between God's call to life and the thrall of death
- conflict between the "already" and the "not yet" of our spiritual condition.

The tone or mood of this section of the service:

- moderate to moderately high energy (leave yourself somewhere to go) OR start with the first "beat" of this section at high energy and then dip slightly
- vocal warmth and intensity stay high through this section

RISING ACTION: Worship continues with the plot's "complication." In this section of a play or worship service, a new element is introduced that changes the action. That is, the direction in which the conflict is developing is changed. In theatre, a series of complications comprise the middle of the play, each one having a beginning, middle, and end of its own and each one revolving around a "discovery." Discoveries may involve facts (new information comes to light), people (a new person enters the scene), or self-insight (a character realizes something important about herself). In *Oedipus the King,* the action changes direction when the facts start coming to light. Oedipus's search for the murderer begins to point toward him.[17] The situation gets "complicated." The plot thickens.

In worship, the discoveries that cause the complication of the service's plot may come in any of these forms, although self-insight may be most common. Again, discovery and complication may occur on any of several levels and be expressed in prayers of confession, prayers of intercession, silence, laments, or meditative hymns. Possible themes include

- inviting God to search our hearts and discovering the depths of our own sinfulness
- examining our lives in the light of God's Word and discovering new dissonances between our life and its values
- confronting our powerlessness over aspects of our own lives and discovering our limits
- recognizing our sinfulness and discovering a need to repent

The tone or mood of this section:

- building energy; it is crucial for this section to keep EITHER a straight strong unbroken line of building momentum OR a carefully planned series of small valleys and larger-and-larger peaks.

130

- no gaps between moves in this section of the service can be tolerated

CLIMAX (or REVERSAL): Aristotle describes the reversal as "a change by which an action veers round to its opposite."[18] This turning point in the action is a result of the building momentum of complications. In *Oedipus the King*, the crisis moment that reverses the action of the play is the moment when Oedipus recognizes that he is the murderer of King Laius.[19]

In worship, reversal occurs in a moment of recognition when we see our situation from God's point of view. Although this often takes place approximately two-thirds of the way through the sermon, it may occur at other times as well.[20] The moment of reversal or recognition might come during the anamnetic section of the Eucharistic prayer, the moment of baptism, an invitational hymn, in a moment of silent reflection, even conceivably, during the offering. The thematic content of such moments will correspond to the "action" of the conflict. For example:

- If the conflict is set in terms of alienation, then the reversal occurs in terms of reconciliation.
- If the conflict is set in terms of the thrall of death, then the reversal occurs in terms of the gift of life.
- If the conflict is set in terms of God's holiness and human sinfulness, then the reversal occurs in terms of forgiveness.

The tone or mood of this section of the service:

- peak intensity is followed immediately by a noticeable drop

DENOUEMENT (or RESOLUTION): This final phase of the worship service's movement runs from the moment of reversal until the benediction. During this portion of a play or worship service, the loose ends are tied up, and whatever is still unresolved in the organizing question is dealt with. The dramatic action slows and the audience or congregation is left with a sense of balance and completion. Closing hymns, pastoral prayers, creeds, and benedictions may help shape the service's denouement. The content of this phase of the action is nearly always a variation on the theme: "let us go out and take this (Good News, peace, salvation, reconciliation, etc.) into the world with us."

The tone or mood of this section of the service:

• the deacceleration may happen quickly or may be meted out more slowly but should never comprise more than 30 percent of the service.

Of the two words that comprise the phrase "dramatic action," the emphasis falls on the second. A strong sense of purpose, of action, of movement undergirds the most effective plots in modern and classic theatre. The people of God should settle for nothing less in their worship. For a service to "feel lively," "move people," or make a difference in the nitty-gritty of peoples' lives, it has to begin with the raw materials of peoples' lives, and "arrange them in a way calculated to have the right effect." That means, at the very least, knowing what conflict gives rise to the movement of the service and knowing how to build that momentum.

BUILDING MOMENTUM

Keeping the service flowing, or momentum building, is the result of doing two things right. First, it is crucial to work with the dramatic action, orchestrating the escalation of intensity in the service through such techniques as vocal effects, musical mood, and speed/frequency of changes (i.e., from prayer to song or song to creed; faster changes create intensity). For example, the Fibinacci theory, a mathematical principle that has been applied to many works of art, suggests that energy builds and compounds in a particular kind of arithmetical progression (the sequence that results from adding a subsequent number and its predecessor in this fashion: 1+2=3, 2+3=5, 3+5=8, etc.) and in keeping with the principle of the Golden Mean. Applying the Fibinacci principle to a sixty-minute period[21] results in segments of increasing length: (3, 5, 8, etc.) which might continue until the climax or reversal (at the point of the Golden Mean) of the service and then diminish in a similar way.

The second method of building momentum is equally important: not dropping the ball. In theatre this is sometimes referred to as not dropping a "beat." Picking up cues, keeping the action moving, keeping the "beats" coming, and being sensitive to the rhythms of the service are important to worship as well. To interrupt flow—to stymie dramatic action—is to risk killing the life of the service. Common interrupters include:

- missed cues that result in gaps between the end of the prayer and the beginning of the hymn, for example.
- responsive readings that drag down the rhythm of the service while doing nothing meaningful to draw people into it. Picking print up off the page with the eyes and running it out one's mouth is no more spiritual an exercise for the folks in the pews than for the one at the lectern.
- the ill-conceived use of silence. Advocates of increasing the church's practice of silence are correct in asserting its potential power. Unfortunately, when placed in the wrong spot, it has as much power to kill momentum as it might have in another moment to build spiritual sensitivity.
- the heavy-handed use of stage directions also interrupts worship's flow, though often the leader intends just the opposite. "Let us pray" is a fine transition from the receiving of the offering to the prayer of dedication; but "Because of all that Christ is to us and has done for us, keeping our minds set on the bounty of our own lives and the needs of others, let us gather our minds and hearts before our God—a God who is merciful and compassionate, who loves a cheerful giver, who is abounding in steadfast love. Remembering that it is a privilege to give tokens of our gratitude to such a God, my friends, let us offer up to God from the rich harvests of our lives our tithes and offerings. Will you please pray with me?" is not. *Because, remember,* and *please* are red flag words in this regard. Compound sentences and abstractions should also give us pause.

Building momentum takes intention, attention, and some effort.

However, it is not as if we are without examples of how it works. The cosmic story of God's way with the world has the strongest plot line ever written. The story that congregations live into and out of every week of their lives is full of conflict and complication and crisis. Building momentum is not so much a question of manufacturing an experience for the congregation and imposing it on them as it is one of being faithful to the shape that life and death conflicts always have. Shape and enlivened performance work together. Why would we want to iron all the bumps out?

••• THE WORSHIP SERVICE AND BLOCKING •••

We do, of course, flatten out the liveliness and dimensionality that strong dramatic action brings to a worship service. Intentionally or unintentionally, in the church we sometimes work against build, momentum, and energy. We compartmentalize and stumble. We interrupt the flow of the worship service. We take it for granted that people will not be carried along by the service; the only question is how long we can hold their attention and how we can get it back once we've lost it.

While there is no substitute for well-conceived dramatic action, physical action has an important supportive role to play in enlivening the service. As Robert Cohen of UC Irvine's drama department says, "By providing a physical enhancement of the dramatic action and lending variety to the play's visual presentation, a good blocking pattern can play a large role in creating theatrical life."[22] Physical action can work *with* the dramatic action of the service and their cooperation can be well managed using *blocking*'s guidelines.

1. *All movement is purposeful and economical.* "Every movement on the stage should mean something,"[23] it is said. We have already explored the *why*s and *wherefore*s of purposeful movement (Habitus #2, chapter 5), but a specific, practical example of those principles at work in the service of worship may be useful here.

I recently spent a day with a group of Doctor of Ministry students working on the use of movement in worship. In the afternoon when the class was nearly over and after I had said, in one gentle way or another, to nearly each and every member of the class that their nervous foot movement was distracting, one brave student asked, "Are you saying we shouldn't move our feet?" The class laughed good-naturedly at my dumbfounded expression. I laughed too, realizing my gentleness had been too gentle and wondering, also, if there was some other reason that they clung to the idea that foot movement was a good thing. Perhaps another teacher had been encouraging them to move? Maybe they believed any movement was better than no movement? Could it be that they thought that foot movement meant the preacher had achieved freedom, was "freed up"?

"I am saying you should only move your feet with purpose. Not out of nervousness, not to expel your own excess energy, not to make yourself feel better. I am saying you should only move your feet when that movement works *with* the direction of the words that are coming out of your mouth at the time. Your feet's job is to communicate to the congregation, not to serve your nervous system."

Of course, whether it is your feet's "job" to communicate to the congregation or not, they will do so. As mentioned earlier, I have heard that Freud said (in the sexist language of his day), "a man cannot lie. If he lies with his lips, he will chatter the truth from his fingertips." An undisciplined preacher's body tells the truth about him or her. The truth about the preacher will out in his or her mannerisms. If you are nervous, it will show in futzy foot movement and balled up hands. A person's nonverbal habits and quirks tell that person's story. The object of disciplining movement in the service of worship is to be able to tell the Gospel story—to do that, it is necessary to put some effort into setting your own story aside.

2. Physical movement works in concert with speech, starting with the thought's impulse and stopping with the thought's end. Movement flows with the direction of the thought or emotion being expressed. More than that, it acts in concordance with it, even punctuating its endings. When crossing the chancel on the line "The Lord is our help in every generation and underneath are the everlasting arms," for example, the performer's feet start moving with the first word and stop cleanly on either the word *generation* or the word *arms*. If they stop on *are* or *everlasting*, the attention of the viewers will be distracted briefly by the uncoupling of the thought's movement and the incarnating physical action, and the impact of the line will be mitigated.

Additionally, it is easy to see how the content of the line might suggest the direction of the movement. It would hardly make non-verbal sense to move from downstage center to a far upstage corner on this line (from the center point of the edge of the platform nearest the audience to the part of the platform farthest from the audience). The action of the line carries the speaker forward toward the one being spoken to. So this line is more likely to be spoken on a cross from, for example, upstage right to downstage center.

BE INTENTIONAL.

3. *Think threes.* Pacing back and forth along the edge of the platform or chancel in front of a congregation is as boring to the eye as a monotone is to the ear. If the incarnational view of preaching being espoused here means anything, it means adding dimensionality to the service of worship. One of the few advantages that live theatre and live worship have over television is that they are three-dimensional. Using only two dimensions (i.e., back and forth pacing) when you have three at your disposal is worse than boring—it's poor stewardship.

To maximize the three-dimensionality of the worship service, move in triangles and arrange groupings of people on the platform in triangles as well. An example of moving in a triangle might look like this:

- start downstage right (the actor's right) and cross left along the edge of the platform or chancel, forming the base of the triangle
- on any acute angle, cross back upstage and to the right, forming the second leg of the triangle.
- close the distance between position 2 and position 1, completing the triangle.

Arranging worship leaders in groups of threes works in a similar way. If, for example, person A is standing downstage center, then person B might stand two or three feet upstage and to the right of A, while person C stands two or three feet upstage and to the left of A. This will be significantly more effective in drawing and holding the congregation's attention than an arrangement that blocks the three worship leaders standing in a straight line.

The rewards for giving this kind of attention to blocking are significant: visual interest is created and the three-dimensionality of embodiment is underscored.

4. Movement trumps anything stationary. A bright red parament, a person speaking in a loud voice, somebody reading the Word of God aloud, a soloist singing, or even a whole choir going all out, can easily be upstaged by somebody walking. The congregation's attention will always be drawn to movement and will always and forever be drawn to movement that suggests that there is something unexpected going on. If there is anything the least bit mysterious about the movement, it will beat out even a phone ringing in the narthex or a baby crying for the congregation's attention.

During much of an average worship service, it would not take even a movement as large as walking to distract the congregation's attention from the speaker. Somebody sitting on the platform (or in the choir, behind the preacher facing the congregation) who simply shifts the gaze from the preacher's face to his or her own lap, may break the momentum the preacher or lay reader is working to create. While it may not be possible or even desirable to control all such movement, it is necessary for worship leaders to be sensitized to the problem.

5. "Selfish Directors" versus "Reliable Interpreters." The phrases are borrowed from the theatre of television. A "selfish director" is a director who prefers to rely on his or her own creative and sometimes idiosyncratic instincts to the point that she or he neglects the very thing the viewer wants to see.

A shot that lingers on the face of one person in a conversation and during which the viewer becomes anxious to see the responder may be the work of a selfish director. A cooking show that relies on long shots and never shows the viewer a close up of what the sauce looks like as it thickens in the pan or the stew that the overhead camera is shooting is another example of selfish directing. In each case the viewers build up a degree of discomfort about what can't be seen and may, in their frustration, even crane their necks.

Colby Lewis, who began his career in theatre and ended teaching radio and TV at Michigan State University, gives this advice to those who would avoid the label *selfish*. "Preserve the nature of your material as faithfully as you can despite its being obliged to pass through your cameras and microphones in order to reach its audience. As superintendent of this translation, you must make yourself a reliable interpreter."[24] The reliable interpreter translates the nature of the Gospel as faithfully as possible, despite its being obliged to pass through human bodies and voices in order to reach its audience.

Just as television must show "what the viewer wants to see" in order to sustain interest, so must worship. When pastors, carried away with the moment or overly confident in their own instincts, lean into an infant baptism, losing the baby in the folds of the Geneva gown or obscuring it behind a raised elbow, they may be guilty of the liturgical equivalent of selfish directing. They have failed to block the scene so that what is most visually compelling can be seen clearly; they have frustrated the congregation's curiosity. (In the case of baptism, this is especially alarming. There is plenty of misconception about the supposed privacy of the act already abroad in the church without reinforcing the notion by effectively leaving the community out!) When the one presiding at the Lord's Table chooses not to break or lift the bread or does so with only the smallest of movements, he or she may be depriving God's people from seeing what they legitimately want to see. Certainly, a pastor who invites the children to sit with him or her on the floor of a chancel that is only a few inches higher than the nave is depriving people of what they want to see. (We will have more to say about blocking children's sermons in the next section.)

6. Reconsider the processional. About eight hundred years before Christ, a Greek chorister stepped out of her place in line at the annual Dionysian festival to say a few words, and theatre was born. But what she stepped out of was by no means nontheatrical. On the contrary, the processional is the oldest of theatrical forms. Peculiarly suited to the church's worship and in popular use since the tenth century church revived theatre for the western world,[25] it is a wonder that recently it has fallen on such hard times. In an age when the church longs for movement, dignity, and majesty in worship, in a time when it is harder and harder to create the electricity which packed sanctuaries used to generate, at a moment in the life of the church when we need to feel like we are going somewhere, the processional bears reconsideration.

From the kind that moves the choir and clergy down the center aisle to the Pentecostal church's "Zion march," processionals afford the average congregation numerous options for embodying the action of the worship service and for drawing worshipers into participation. There is an electricity in the act of human faces and bodies parading that cannot be achieved by any number of loud voices or bright colors. At the same time, the processional provides an infinitely flexible form for such an experience. It is easily adaptable to liturgical flavors, cultural sensibilities, and thematic content. Processionals can be hierarchical or non, formal or in, and playful or stately, for example. What they cannot be is replaced by anything stationary.

Plot, no matter how well-conceived, and blocking, no matter how well-executed, cannot create life for a worship service. Only the Holy Spirit can do that. However it is up to the human beings involved to create an environment in which worshipers can open themselves to the Spirit's movement. When physical movement and a strong sense of dramatic action work together in a service, the human heart is tuned to expect movement, its strings are poised to resonate with it, and its feet are made ready to follow.

✦✦✦ MAKING SPACE ✦✦✦

Opening oneself to the movement of the Holy Spirit implies not only readiness to move but space to do it. Most often such a response is made in figurative space-psychic space. However, literal, physical space affects figurative space in some surprising ways. In worship, space is a product of the demands of aesthetic distance (discussed in chapter 2) and action. Worship that moves purposefully in and through physical space is incarnational worship—bumpy with dimensionality—and more likely to be lively than flat. Space is what makes bodies and physicality possible. Much of what is important about the use of space in worship has been explored—directly or by implication—in the preceding section. However, one major area of interest remains.

Contemporary worship could learn much from Thornton Wilder, that genius of modern American theatre who is known for, among other things, making space. His sets are often only chairs, maybe a simple table, with everything else suggested in pantomime. Think of the stripped-down look of *Our Town* (1938). Its set, as well as such sets as *Pullman Car Hiawatha* and *Happy Journey to Trenton*, are aimed, Wilder says, at "capturing not verisimilitude but reality."[26]

Wilder discovered that staging theatre in a "showcase" or a "box set," which was loaded with specific objects (furniture, props, and other knick-knacks designed to literally reproduce the look of a Victorian drawing room, for example), fixed and narrowed the play to one moment in time, working against its ability to raise the action of the play "into the realm of idea and type and universal."[27] It is this raising of individual action into the realm of the universal that constitutes the power of theatre (and, in part, of worship). Wilder believed that to work against it was to "draw [theatre's] teeth." "When you emphasize *place* in the theatre, you drag down and limit and harness time to it. You thrust the action back into past time, whereas it is precisely the glory of the stage that it is always 'now' there."[28]

"Nowness" is a glory of the worship service as well. It is in the here and now, in your heart and mine, that the Spirit moves. It is through this very room where we are sitting that salvific action sweeps. Worship can only be present-tense. Even anamnetic activity draws the past *into the present*. If we wish for worshipers to have a here-and-now experience, we would do well to heed Wilder's advice and clear the stage.

••• Using Space •••

The Use of Props

A practical application of Wilder's rule may be made to the use of objects in the service of worship. Take, for example, the following scene: A preacher starts her sermon, holding an apple. She talks about how lovely it looks, how anxious she is to bite into it. She takes a bite. She tells the congregation that she has discovered that it is rotten.

As an opening gambit for a sermon, it is not bad. Everybody can identify with the experience, there is a certain sensory appeal, and the use of the prop adds a bit of novelty. But consider the question of what the preacher has gained in the use of the literal apple that could not be as well or better accomplished with word pictures and the listener's mental motion picture screen. And consider the possibility that in narrowing the focus to one specific apple (an apple that is hard to see for the folks who are sitting farther back than the second pew) and in doing the listeners' imaginative work for them she has lost something as well.

There is a "dragging" effect, to use Wilder's word, to a prop used in this way. The use of one small apple may not constitute "the loading of the stage with specific objects" or jerk the listeners out of the present, but it does pull them just one step away from *experiencing* their own present and one step closer to *thinking* about the nature of apples and the neatness of the analogy. Wilder's rule applies to this case in a general way: objects have the power to focus OR to narrow our experience in space and time.

The trick is knowing when a prop focuses and draws us in and when it narrows and drags us down. Generally speaking, props have less drawing power than we give them credit for. In addition, worship leaders tend to underestimate the potential for distraction that occurs in the handling of a prop. How and when a prop is picked up, held, and put down involve the same complicated and potentially disastrous issues as the futzy foot problem or the worship leader who moves while somebody else is talking. Though well-handled, well-chosen props may occasionally add to a service of worship, the risk in using them is high for all but the most disciplined performer.

CREATING LEVELS

One way to make more literal space in worship is to add levels— platforms, risers, raked seating, chancel stairs, etc. Not only do levels open the chancel for movement, they make sightlines work and create visual interest. Levels are the key to solving that most common of all sightline problems, the children's sermon. If the children are invited forward to sit on a set of risers pulled out just for them, or on two or three 4-foot by 4-foot by 2 1/2-foot platforms arranged for them ahead of time, or to a couple of benches that are added to the top and second steps of the chancel stairs as the children come down the aisle, the congregation is more likely to actually be able to see the pastor interact with the children.[29] Similarly, levels and thrust staging can be the solution to the second-most common problem in using worship space, that of the preacher who wants to be closer to the congregation.

USING THE FURNITURE

In many chancels there are set pieces of furniture that may either enable or impede movement through space. A fixed pulpit, a heavy table, or a built-in choir stall can be obstacles or touchstones in blocking movement. Whether or not they constitute "sacred space" varies from tradition to tradition. Yes for Roman Catholics, no for the Reformed churches.

Even when the pulpit and table (or altar) are not officially considered sacred space, it is most dramatically effective to treat them as separate space—that is, space with a specialized function, which has absorbed a kind of symbolic "heft" over the years. This is a practice that is especially congenial to the Reformed tradition's understanding of space that is "set apart" from a common to a sacred use. However, even in non-liturgical (or anti-liturgical!) churches, the pulpit projects a certain ambience. Not just anybody should stand there in not just any way. Even in nonsacramental churches there is a feeling of reverence for the table upon which the Lord's Supper is laid. Like Bibles, baptismal fonts, and chalices, the larger pieces of furniture have an aura of sacredness and seem to demand respect.

Honoring such demands makes for good theatre. The pulpit is reserved for a certain kind of activity or a certain moment in the flow of the service—its symbolic power is not diluted by using it casually or because it is the only place from which a person can be seen. Though the table may be movable, it too has a distinct role to play. It is not furniture to be leaned on or stumbled against. We know where it is and why it is there and we pay respect to it by moving around it with awareness and purpose.

It is not that we believe that furniture generates force-fields of holy energy, it is that it looks that way to the congregation. They may not believe it either, but the most rational worshiper would squirm if the pulpit Bible were dropped and stepped on, if a rat were found drinking out of the baptismal font, or if a barefooted painter used the table for a stepstool.

✦✦✦ Performing the Word ✦✦✦

The thing I miss most about the Pentecostal church of my youth is not the ecstatic speech, it is the singing. In my mind's eye, I see Buddy Ellison on a humid Sunday evening, urging us on. "This time sing those words like you really believe them!" He waves his plumber's arms, inclines his head; his face glows. Hands are raised all over the room, hearts are focused on that inner reality—very inner. Yet we are together in our leaning—leaning into the holy, leaning into the mystery. And, eyes closed, we sing the words as if we really mean them.

Performing the word implies just that kind of being present in the words. It is almost too weak a thing to say that such activity has "drawing power" or that "one of its characteristics is its participatory nature." In the face of those kinds of worship experiences, it seems obvious that words are incarnated in human body and voice—that the self-giving involved in the process has a transformative effect. It seems almost silly to say it out loud. If you have experienced it, you know it. If you have experienced it, you may need only a slight reminder, the kind that Buddy Ellison used to give that small New Jersey congregation weekly.

It is the goal of this book to give a slight reminder of how it is that the Word of God is communicated—of how the Word is performed in the lives of people of faith two millenia after Jesus first incarnated it. If you were to witness such an event next Saturday night from your balcony aisle seat or some Sunday morning from your spot on the eighth pew, what would it be like? I believe it would have the ring of Truth about it, and that it would look somehow, strangely familiar. Oh, so familiar.

The preacher has often been compared with the actor... There is a real point of analogy. The actor creates a part, as the phrase is; but it is only by appropriating a personality which the dramatist really created and put into his hands. And that is what the preacher has to do... (she or he) has to interpret Christ.[30]

The Word

by Helen Kromer

I open my mouth to speak
And the word is there,
Formed by the lips, the tongue,
The organ of voice. Formed by the brain,
Transmitting the word
By breath.

I open my mouth to speak
And the word is there,
Caught by the organ of hearing, the ear.
Transmitting the thought to the brain
Through the Word.

Just so do we communicate—
You and I: the thought
From one mind leaping to another,
Given shape and form and substance,
So that we know and are known
Through the Word.

But let me speak to my very small son
And the words mean nothing,
For he does not know my language.
So I must show him: "This is your foot,"
I say; "It is meant for walking."
I help him up. "Here is the way to walk!"
And one day, "walking" shapes in his brain
With the word.

God had something to say to [us]
But the words meant nothing,
For we did not know [God's] language.
And so we were shown: "Behold, the Man,"
[God] said. "This is the image, the thought
In my mind—[Humankind] as I mean [you],
   loving and serving.
I have put Him in flesh. Now the Word
Has shape and form and substance
To travel between us. Let Him show forth love
Till one day 'loving' shapes in your brain
With the Word."[31]

Notes

Chapter One

1. Amos Wilder, "Electric Chimes and Ram's Horns," *Christian Century* 88, no. 4 (27 January 1971): 105.

2. Richard Lischer, *A Theology of Preaching: The Dynamics of the Gospel* (Nashville: Abingdon Press, 1981), 14-16.

3. Lucy Rose, *Sharing the Word: Preaching in the Roundtable Church* (Louisville: Westminster/John Knox Press, 1997), 89-118.

4. Wade Clark Roof, *A Generation of Seekers: The Spiritual Journeys of the Baby Boom Generation* (San Francisco: HarperSanFrancisco, 1993) 169-71.

5. Thomas Troeger, *Ten Strategies for Preaching in a Multi-Media Culture* (Nashville: Abingdon Press, 1996), 8-16.

6. Charles L. Bartow, *God's Human Speech: A Practical Theology of Proclamation* (Grand Rapids: Eerdmans, 1997) represents a post-liberal response to postmodernism. Alternative responses are explored in Ronald J. Allen, Barbara Shires Blaisdell, and Scott Black Johnston, *Theology for Preaching: Authority, Truth, and Knowledge of God in a Postmodern Ethos* (Nashville: Abingdon Press, 1997).

7. Charles L. Bartow, *The Preaching Moment: A Guide to Sermon Delivery* (Nashville: Abingdon Press, 1980), 18.

8. Leonora Tubbs Tisdale explores the nature of preaching as "a highly contextual act of theological construction in the congregational context" (p. 30) in *Preaching as Local Theology and Folk Art* (Minneapolis: Fortress Press, 1997).

9. Fred B. Craddock, *As One Without Authority* (Enid, Okla.: Phillips University Press, 1974), 21.

10. William J. Carl, *Preaching Christian Doctrine* (Philadelphia: Fortress Press, 1984) 139-158. The appendix contains three examples of such doctrinal preaching.

147

Notes

11. Dorothy Sayers, *Mind of the Maker* (San Francisco: Harper and Row, 1941).

12. See for example the account of Tillich's lecture given at the Museum of Modern Art in New York City, February 17, 1959. *Cross Currents* 10 (Winter 1960): 1-14 or his chapter on Protestant attitudes toward the arts, "Protestantism and Artistic Style" in *Theology and Culture*, ed. Robert C. Kimball (New York: Oxford Press, 1959).

13. Jürgen Moltmann, *The Theology of Play*, trans. Reinhard Ulrich (New York: Harper and Row, 1972).

14. A comprehensive treatment of the connections between theological categories and performance art is made by Alla Bozarth-Campbell in *The Word's Body: An Incarnational Aesthetic of Interpretation* (Tuscaloosa: University of Alabama Press, 1979). For theological analysis of visual arts, see John Dillenberger, *A Theology of Artistic Sensibilities: The Visual Arts and the Church* (New York: Crossroad, 1986).

15. H. H. Farmer, *The Servant of the Word* (Philadelphia: Fortress Press, 1942), 67.

16. These categories are suggested by Richard Lischer in *A Theology of Preaching*, chapter 1, and by P. T. Forsyth in *Positive Preaching and the Modern Mind* (Grand Rapids: Baker Book House, 1980), 41-45.

17. John Updike, "Seven Stanzas at Easter," in *Collected Poems 1953-1993* (New York: Alfred A. Knopf, 1995), 20-21.

18. Yngve Brilioth, *A Brief History of Preaching* (Philadelphia: Fortress Press, 1965), 46.

19. Augustine, *On Christian Doctrine* in *Select Library of Nicean and Post-Nicean Fathers of the Christian Church*, vol. III, ed. P. Schaff (Grand Rapids: Eerdmans, 1956), 594.

20. Richard Lischer, *Theories of Preaching: Selected Readings in the Homiletical Tradition* (Durham, N.C.: Labyrinth Press, 1987), 9.

21. J. H. Nichols, *History of Christianity, 1650-1950* (New York: Ronald Press, 1956), 29.

22. Guilielumus Baum, Eduardus Cunitz and Eduardus Ruess, ed. *Corpus Reformatum: Ioannis Calvini Opera Quae Supesunt Omnia* (Brunsrigae, Calif.: Schwetschke et Filium, 1897), 713.

23. DeWitte T. Holland, *The Preaching Tradition: A Brief History* (Nashville: Abingdon Press, 1980), 42.

24. Harry S. Stout, *The New England Soul: Preaching and Religious Culture in Colonial New England* (New York: Oxford University Press, 1986), 40-41.

25. Holland, *The Preaching Tradition*, 56

26. Stout, *The New England Soul*, 206

27. P. T. Forsyth, "The Moralization of Religion," *London Quarterly Review* 128: 172.

28. Many late-twentieth-century homileticians may be mentioned as representative of this view. For a helpful account of this period see Lucy Rose, *Sharing the Word*, 60-62.

Chapter Two

1. Susanne K. Langer, *Feeling and Form* (New York: Charles Scribner's Sons, 1953), 40.

2. Langer, *Feeling and Form*, 398-99.

3. Ibid, 49.

4. Charles Rice on preaching as art in *Concise Encyclopedia of Preaching*, ed. William Willimon and Richard Lischer (Louisville: Westminster John Knox Press, 1995), 17.

5. M. James Young, lecture on "Church and Theatre," Wheaton, Ill., 1975.

6. Arthur Hopkins, *How's Your Second Act?* (New York: Samuel French, 1948), 8.

7. Francis Fergusson, *The Idea of a Theatre: A Study of Ten Plays* (Garden City, N.Y.: Doubleday, 1949), 8.

Notes

8. Richard Boleslavsky, *Acting: the First Six Lessons* (New York: Theatre Arts, 1933/1973), 56-57.

9. *Arrested performance* is a term used for written texts, by Beverly Whitaker Long and Mary Frances Hopkins, *Performing Literature: An Introduction to Oral Interpretation* (Englewood Cliffs, N. J.: Prentice-Hall, 1982), 2.

10. "On the Spectacles" in *Dramatic Theory and Criticism: Greeks to Growtowski,* ed. Bernard F. Dukore (New York: Holt, Rinehart & Winston, 1974), 93.

11. Eugene Lowry, "Narrative Preaching" in *Concise Encyclopedia of Preaching,* 342.

12. Charles L. Rice, *Interpretation and Imagination* (Philadelphia: Fortress Press, 1970), 25.

13. Don Wardlaw, "Preaching as Lived Experience," course handout, McCormick Theological Seminary, Chicago, Ill.

14. P. T. Forsyth, *Positive Preaching and the Modern Mind* (1907; Grand Rapids: Baker Book House, 1980), 349.

15. Victor Turner, *From Ritual to Theatre: The Human Seriousness of Play* (New York: PAJ Publishing, 1982), 104.

16. See, for example, Jerzy Growtowski, *Towards a Poor Theatre* (New York: Simon & Schuster, 1968) and Peter Brook, *The Empty Space* (New York: Macmillan, 1978).

17. Alla Bozarth-Campbell, *The Word's Body: An Incarnational Aesthetic of Interpretation* (Tuscaloosa: University of Alabama, 1979), 86.

18. Oscar G. Brockett, *The Essential Theatre* (New York: Holt, Rinehart & Winston, 1980), 10.

19. Thornton Wilder, *Three Plays by Thornton Wilder* (New York: Harper and Row, 1958), vii.

20. Ibid., viii.

21. Ibid., x.

22. Turner, *From Ritual to Theatre,* 86.

23. Richard Ward, *Speaking from the Heart: Preaching with Passion* (Nashville: Abingdon Press, 1992), 77.

24. Henri Bergson, *The Creative Mind,* trans. Mabelle L. Andison (New York: Philosophical Library, 1946), 101-2. Quoted in Don Geiger, *The Sound, Sense and Performance of Literature* (Chicago: Scott Foresman & Company, 1963), 17.

25. Charles L. Bartow, "Toward a Rhetoric of the Word" (manuscript, San Anselmo, Calif., 1984), 2.

26. Norman Jeffares, "W. B. Yeats and His Method of Writing Verse" in *The Performance of Yeats,* ed. J. Hall and M. Steinman (New York: P. F. Collier and Son, 1961), 271. Quoted in Geiger, 18-19.

27. Robert Beloof, *The Performing Voice in Literature* (Boston: Little, Brown and Co., 1966), 11.

28. Ibid.

29. Richard Boleslavsky, *Acting: The First Six Lessons* (New York: Theatre Arts, 1933), 206.

30. Bozarth understands incarnation as "the coming together of poem as a real being and interpreter as a real being in order to create a new being, in which the integrity of each is still preserved." Bozarth-Campbell, *The Word's Body,* 2.

31. Arthur Hopkins, *How's Your Second Act?* (New York: Samuel French, 1948), 15.

Chapter Three

1. Albert Mehrabian, *Silent Messages: Implicit Communication of Emotions and Attitudes* (Belmont, Calif.: Wadsworth Publishing, 1971), 43-44.

2. This may account for the wide use of the word "listener" in homiletical literature. That the term is preferred to "viewer" is not surprising, given the priority of speech in preaching. This priority has been challenged recently by Kathy Black, *A Healing Homiletic: Preaching and Disability* (Nashville: Abingdon Press, 1996).

3. Patsy Rodenburg, *The Right to Speak: Working with the Voice* (New York: Routledge, Chapman & Hall, 1992), 86.

4. Kristin Linklater, *Freeing the Natural Voice* (New York: Drama Book Specialists, 1976), 184.

5. The role of the "mask" on sinus cavities is debatable. While the notion of the "mask" has been helpful to many singers, it is not clear whether the sinuses actually contribute to vocal resonance.

6. See, for example, Ralph R. Leutenegger, *The Sounds of American English* (Scott Foresman & Company, 1963).

7. See, for example, G. Robert Jacks, *Getting the Word Across* (Grand Rapids: Eerdmans Press, 1995) for a full range of diagnostic, therapeutic and oral interpretation helps. See also Rodenburg, *The Right to Speak*, for work on the psychology of voice, and Jon Eisenson, *Voice and Diction: A Program for Improvement* (New York: Macmillan, 1985), for work on the mechanics of diction and vocal production.

8. Constantin Stanislavski, *An Actor Prepares* (New York: Theatre Arts, 1936), 92.

9. As taught by M. James Young, Wheaton College, Wheaton, Ill.

Chapter Four

1. Leland Powers, *Practice Book* (Boston: Haven Merrill Powers Publishers, 1916), ix-x.

2. Constantin Stanislavski, *Building a Character* (New York: Theatre Arts, 1949), 143.

3. I have adapted and extended Powers' theory, renaming the categories to better suit contemporary sensibilities.

4. H. H. Farmer, *The Servant of the Word* (Philadelphia: Fortress Press, 1942), 39-40.

5. Arthur Hopkins, *How's Your Second Act?* (New York: Samuel French, 1948), 10.

6. Ibid., 42.

7. Stanislavski, *Building a Character*, 242.

8. Alla Bozarth-Campbell, *The Word's Body: An Incarnational Aesthetic of Interpretation* (Tuscaloosa: University of Alabama, 1979), 138.

9. Ibid.

Chapter Five

1. Marsh Cassady, *Acting, Step by Step* (San Jose, Calif.: Resource Publications, 1988), 2.

2. Viola Spolin, *Improvisation for the Theater* (Evanston, Ill.: Northwestern University Press, 1983), 3.

3. Julia Cameron, *The Artist's Way: A Spiritual Path to Higher Creativity* (New York: Jeremy P. Tarcher, 1992), 2.

4. Jürgen Moltmann, *Theology of Play*, trans. Reinhard Ulrich (New York: Harper & Row, 1972).

5. Johan Huizinga, *Homo Ludens* (Boston: Beacon Press, 1950), 28.

6. Anne C. Roark, "The Secrets of Creativity," in the *Los Angeles Times*, November 12, 1989, 12.

7. Ibid.

Notes

8. Alla Bozarth-Campbell, *The Word's Body: An Incarnational Aesthetic of Interpretation* (Tuscaloosa: University of Alabama, 1979), 79.

9. Arthur Hopkins, *How's Your Second Act?* (New York: Samuel French, 1948), 8.

10. Constantin Stanislavski, *An Actor Prepares* (New York: Theatre Arts, 1936), 76-77.

11. Viola Spolin, *Improvisation for the Theater* (Chicago: Northwestern University Press, 1983), 174.

12. Advanced actors may also do this exercise in triads.

13. Translated by Mark Schmidt and arranged by Molly Day Thacher from Chekov's 1922 notes. Quoted in Toby Cole, *Acting, A Handbook of the Stanislavski Method* (New York: Crown Publishing Group, 1955), 139.

14. Stanislavski, *An Actor Prepares*, 86.

15. Quoted in Cameron, *The Artist's Way*, 22.

16. Stanislavski, *An Actor Prepares*, 87.

17. Cameron, *The Artist's Way*, 20-21.

18. Spolin, *Improvisation for the Theater*, 170.

19. Richard Lischer, *A Theology of Preaching: The Dynamics of the Gospel* (Nashville: Abingdon Press, 1981), 19.

20. Cole, *Acting*, 137.

21. Cassady, *Acting, Step by Step*, 36.

22. Paul Scott Wilson argues that imagination is best understood as a function of language. In his view "polarities in language," which may or may not be associated with mental images, release imagination. *Imagination of the Heart: New Understandings in Preaching* (Nashville: Abingdon Press, 1988), 32-33.

23. Actually, the term used by Stanislavski for the motivations that drive the character and the play forward is "objectives." There has been much confusion over the seeming dryness of this word. See Richard Brestoff for a helpful reframing of this concept in terms of "images." *The Great Acting Teachers and Their Methods* (Lyme, N.H.: Smith and Kraus, 1995), 49.

24. As advocated by Natalie Goldberg, *Writing Down the Bones* (Boston: Shambhala, 1986), 8, and Julia Cameron, *The Artist's Way* (New York: G. P. Putnam's Sons, 1992), 9-18.

25. Perhaps the most famous example of this technique in contemporary homiletics is found in "Doxology," a sermon by Fred Craddock in *As One Without Authority* (Enid, Okla.: Phillips University Press, 1974), where Craddock portrays an idea as an animal.

26. Eric Bentley, *The Life of Drama* (London: Methuen and Co., 1965), 169.

27. Ibid., 166-68.

28. See G. Robert Jacks, *Getting the Word Across* (Grand Rapids: Eerdmans, 1994), 37-44, for a full description of the use of eye contact in reading Scripture.

29. Hopkins, *How's Your Second Act?*, 43.

30. Ibid., 14-15.

31. Ibid., 15.

32. Ibid., 17.

33. Cicely Berry, *The Actor and the Text* (New York: Applause Theatre Books, 1992), 19.

Chapter Six

1. Henning Tenger, "Kierkegaard as Falsifier of History" in *Modern Critical Views: Soren Kierkegaard,* ed. Harold Bloom (New York: Chelsea House, 1989), 165.

2. Søren Kierkegaard, *Purity of Heart*, trans. Douglas V. Steere (New York: Harper & Row, 1938), 179-82.

3. Richard Ward, *Speaking from the Heart* (Nashville: Abingdon Press, 1992), 77.

4. Arthur Hopkins, *How's Your Second Act?* (New York: Samuel French, 1948), 8.

5. James Carey, "A Cultural Approach to Communication," *Communication* 12, no. 1 (December, 1975): 1-22.

6. Alla Bozarth-Campbell, *The Word's Body: An Incarnational Aesthetic of Interpretation* (Tuscaloosa: University of Alabama, 1979), 131-32.

7. O. B. Hardison, Jr., *Christian Rite and Christian Drama in the Middle Ages* (Baltimore: Johns Hopkins Press, 1965), 40.

8. Richard Schechner, "From Ritual to Theatre and Back" in *Ritual, Play and Performance*, ed. Richard Schechner and Mady Schuman (New York: Seabury Press, 1976), 210-11.

9. Ibid., 211.

10. Constantin Stanislavski, *An Actor Prepares* (New York: Theatre Arts, 1946), 236-38 (Emphasis added).

11. Francis Ferguson's introduction to Aristotle's *Poetics* (New York: Hill and Wang, 1961), 8.

12. Aristotle, *Poetics* VI.6, trans. S. H. Butcher with introduction by Francis Ferguson (New York: Hill & Wang, 1961).

13. *Poetics*, VII.3.

14. Eric Bentley, *The Life of Drama* (London: Methuen and Co., 1965), 15.

15. E. M. Forster, *Aspects of the Novel*, quoted in Bentley, p.15.

16. Oscar G. Brockett, *The Essential Theatre* (New York: Holt, Rinehart & Winston, 1980), 25.

17. Brockett, *The Essential Theatre*, 26.

18. *Poetics*, XI.1.

19. Brockett, *The Essential Theatre*, 26.

20. The time-honored principle of the Golden Mean suggests that the climax of a dramatic work will occur at the point that is 61.8% of the way through the work. (Golden Mean principle: smaller B is to larger A as A is to the sum of its parts.)

21. See David C. Dikau and Robert Allan Petker, *Choral Questions and Answers*, vol. III (Palo Alto: Pavan Publishers, 1992), 7-8 for an application of the Fibinacci principle to rehearsal periods.

22. Robert Cohen, *Theatre: Brief Edition* (Palo Alto: Mayfield Publishing Co., 1983), 157.

23. Hopkins, 15.

24. Colby Lewis, *The TV Director/Interpreter* (New York: Hastings House Publishers, 1974), 136.

25. For a helpful history of the theatre and its relationship with liturgical drama, see Oscar G. Brockett, *History of the Theatre* (Boston: Allyn and Bacon, 1987).

26. Thornton Wilder, *Three Plays by Thornton Wilder* (New York: Bantam Books, 1958), xi.

27. Ibid., x.

28. Ibid.

29. This does not deal, of course, with the larger issue of how the seeing of the children is used in the worship service, about whether the children's cuteness is being exploited or legitimately enjoyed.

30. P. T. Forsyth, *Positive Preaching and the Modern Mind* (Grand Rapids: Baker Book House, 1980), 90.

31. From *For Heaven's Sake: A Musical Revue*. Book and lyrics by Helen Kromer, Music by Frederick Silver (Boston: Baker's Plays, 1963), 18-19.

Printed in the United States
23242LVS00005B/448-471